THE INTERACTIVE
DINOSAUR
ENCYCLOPEDIA

igloobooks

igloobooks

Published in 2013
by Igloo Books Ltd
Cottage Farm
Sywell
NN6 0BJ
www.igloobooks.com

SHE001 0713
2 4 6 8 10 9 7 5 3 1
ISBN 978-1-78197-542-8

Printed and manufactured in China

CONTENTS

Interactive Instructions

On your mobile, or tablet device, download the **FREE** Layar App.

Look out for the **SCAN ME** logo and scan the whole page.

Unlock, discover and enjoy the enhanced content.

For more details, visit: **www.igloobooks.com**

DINOSAUR TIMELINE

Massive volcanic eruptions cause mass extinctions, wiping out 90% of marine life and 70% of land life!

First dinosaurs evolve. They are mostly fairly small (no more than 20 ft or 6m), bipedal and fast moving. Marine reptiles like Icthyosaurs and Plesiosaurs also evolve at this time.

Dinosaurs dominant. First mammals evolve.

Mesozoic era

248 – 65 Million Years Ago

Triassic period	Jurassic period
248 – 206 Million Years Ago	206 – 144 Million Years Ago

Stegosaurus

Eoraptor
Coelophysis

Compsognathus
Diplodocus
Brachiosaurus

Sauropsids such as the archosaurs dominate. First cynodonts evolve.

Apatosaurus
Kentrosaurus
Seismosaurus
Allosaurus

Megalosaurus

Age of dinosaurs.
Dinosaurs are at their
peak in size, variety
and numbers
and dominate every
continent.

K-T extinction.
End of the
dinosaurs.

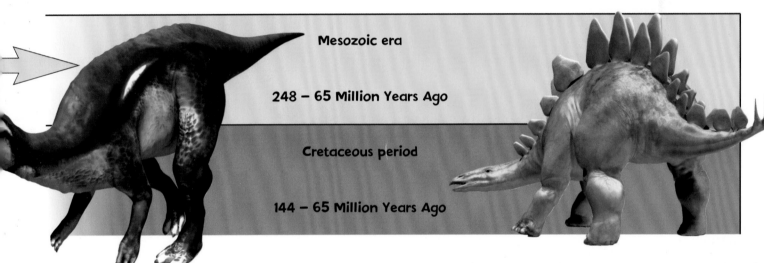

Mesozoic era

248 – 65 Million Years Ago

Cretaceous period

144 – 65 Million Years Ago

Hadrosaurus
Velociraptor
Protoceratops

Centrosaurus
Troodon
Tyrannosaurus
Triceratops
Ankylosaurus
Edmontosaurus

Giganotosaurus
Spinosaurus

Argentinosaurus
Nodosaurus

Deinonychus

Acrocanthosaurus

Iguanadon

Baryonyx

INTRODUCTION

The world we all live in today will change in your lifetime, and if you ask your parents and grandparents, they will tell you how much it has changed in their lifetime. Humans have spread across the Earth and we have colonized and visited virtually all of the land mass available on our planet. We are continuing to explore to the very bottom of our oceans and even beyond our own planet. We have explored our Moon and now we are beginning to explore other planets such as Mars, Venus and beyond.

However, although it is true that we humans have had phenomenal success during our time on Earth, it is also true that the Earth is a lot, lot older than us. Our time on Earth is absolutely tiny when we compare it to the total amount of time there has been life on Earth.

The Earth is about 4.5 billion years old but humans have lived on Earth for only 250,000 years of that time. Or to put it another way, if you stretch out your arm and fingers and then look at the length of your arm from your shoulder all the way to your fingers, then the very, very tip of the fingernail on your longest finger represents how long we have been here. If you take a nail file and scrape off the tip of the fingernail, then you have just wiped out the existence of humans on planet Earth.

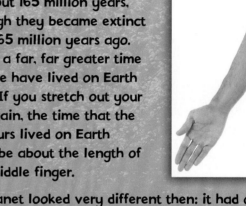

Dinosaurs lived on Earth for about 165 million years, although they became extinct about 65 million years ago. That is a far, far greater time than we have lived on Earth so far. If you stretch out your arm again, the time that the dinosaurs lived on Earth would be about the length of your middle finger.

Our planet looked very different then: it had one large land mass (or continent) called Pangaea.

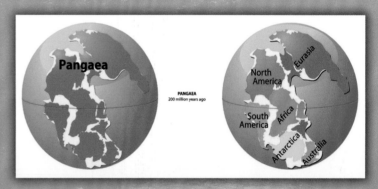

Because dinosaurs died out a long time ago, our knowledge of them can only be gained from the fossils we've found. Advances in modern technology, such as MRI scans and high powered x-rays have revealed much more information about the fossils already discovered, as have advances in our studies of animal and reptile behaviour.

In this book, we will help you try and answer
your questions about dinosaurs. What did they
look like? What did they eat? Did some dinosaurs eat
other dinosaurs? Which dinosaur was the biggest? How big
was it? Which was the smallest? How did they move? Which
ones were fast? Which ones were slow? And what happened
to them? When we did we find the first fossils? Where are
most of the fossils found now? We will answer all of these
questions and many more. We will look at a large range
of dinosaurs and give you the stats and details of each
dinosaur, as well as tell you what myths and facts about
dinosaurs are true. And we'll probably give you some
amazing facts and information that you didn't know.

ANCESTORS OF THE DINOSAURS

Dinosaurs weren't the first reptiles to rule the earth and in the next few pages you will see some of the reptiles that existed before the dinosaurs.

INTRODUCING ...

ERYOPS

DIMETRODON

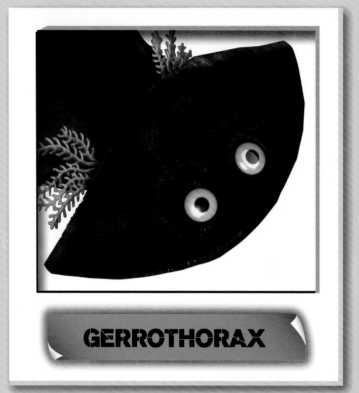

GERROTHORAX

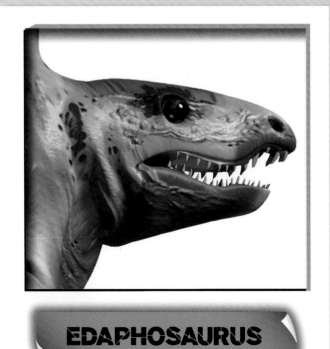

EDAPHOSAURUS

ERYOPS

Eryops was one of the largest animals of its time, measuring 5–6 ft (1.5–2.0 m) long, and lived during the Permian period, roughly 270 million years ago, long before dinosaurs. It was a fierce amphibian, living in swamps and along rivers and probably would have resembled a modern-day alligator.

SUPER FACT

Eryops had a primitive ear which allowed it to hear airborne sounds.

DID YOU KNOW?

Eryops, pronounced Ar-ee-ops, means ´drawn out face´, it was named in 1887 by Edward Drinker Cope, an American scientist.

GUESS WHAT

Eryops was a meat-eater and very strong. It had thick, strong bones, four powerful legs and a short tail. It moved very slowly on land because of its bulky body and short legs. Eryops ate mostly fish, small reptiles and other amphibians.

WOW, REALLY?

Eryops grabbed prey and then threw its head up and tossed the meat backwards and deep into its mouth.

GERROTHORAX

Gerrothorax looked a lot like a giant 3.3 ft (1 m) long tadpole. Its a type of **plagiosaurid** and it lived 200 million years ago, in lakes and rivers, feeding on small animals. This rather strange animal was a meat-eater and probably lay at the bottom of lakes, scanning for prey with its mouth open ready to catch them.

AWESOME FACT

Modern amphibians lose their gills when they grow older but Gerrothorax didn't. It had three pairs of gills throughout its life, meaning it could live in water as an adult.

WOW, REALLY?

Gerrothorax's eyes were very close-set on the top of its head so it could only look upwards, so it would not have been able to see anything swimming underneath it.

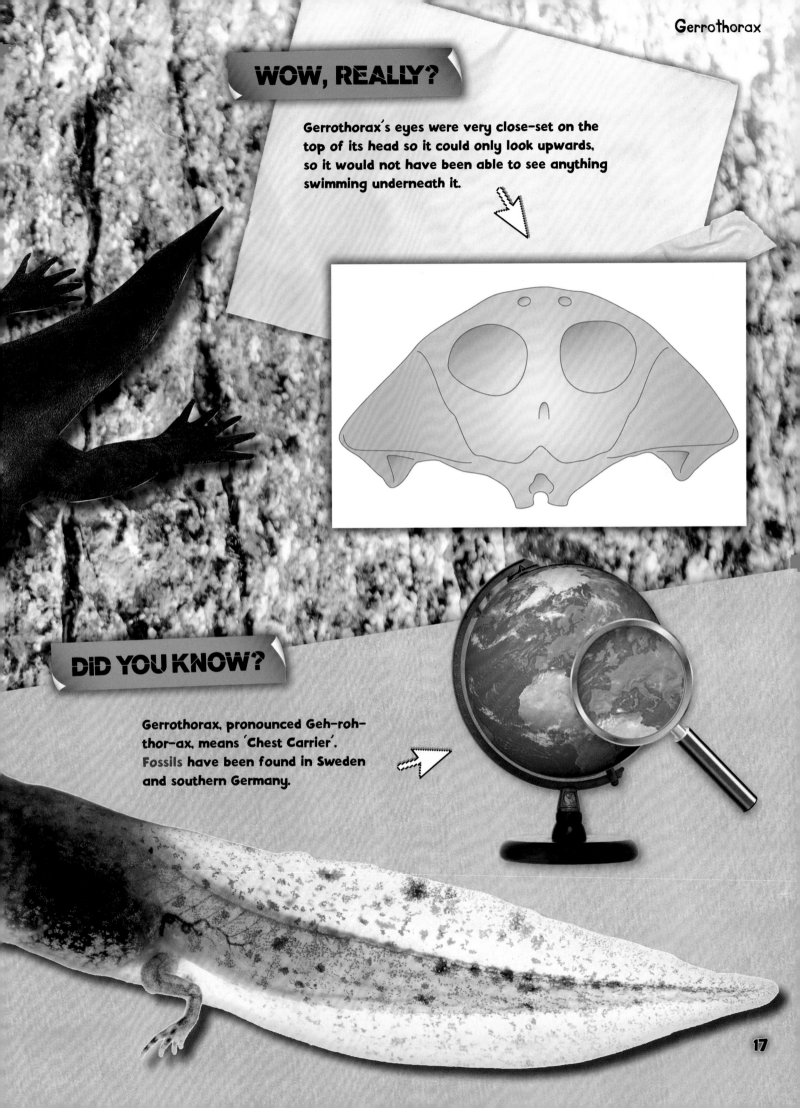

DID YOU KNOW?

Gerrothorax, pronounced Geh-roh-thor-ax, means 'Chest Carrier'. Fossils have been found in Sweden and southern Germany.

DIMETRODON

Dimetrodon was a sail-backed, meat-eating animal that lived during the Permian Period, roughly 280 million years ago, long before the dinosaurs evolved. When it was alive, deserts covered much of the Earth. Dimetrodon was suited to living in hot, dry conditions. Dimetrodon was believed to be very fierce and have no predators. Fossilized skeletons indicate that this creature could be as big as 11.5 ft (3.5 m) long and probably weighed about 550 lbs (250 kg). Dimetrodon walked on four legs that sprawled out to the sides, unlike the dinosaurs, whose legs extended under their bodies. It is likely it was a very fast runner.

AWESOME

The Dimetrodon used its distinctive sail to soak up valuable sunlight during the daytime, and control the heat of the body. It was also used to frighten other species.

HOW DO YOU SAY MY NAME?

di-met-ro-don

WOW, AMAZING

Dimetrodon had two types of teeth. Long teeth at the front to cut through meat and shorter ones at the back to tear the meat into small pieces.

DID YOU KNOW?

Many people think that the Dimetrodon was a dinosaur. However, they lived tens of millions of years before the first dinosaurs had even evolved. The Dimetrodon is probably more closely related to humans than to the dinosaurs. It is a pelycosaur, which had many mammal-like characteristics and is the relative of warm-blooded mammals.

EDAPHOSAURUS

Edaphosaurus was one of the earliest known plant-eaters, and looked similar to Dimetrodon because of the sail along its back, but it was generally smaller. This reptile lived on land, roughly 320 million years ago. We still know very little about the Edaphosaurus, as the only fossils that have ever been found consisted of a few fragments of its skeleton, including some of its spines. Edaphosaurus lived in the swamps of North America and Western Europe.

Like the Dimetrodon, the Edaphosaurus was a pelycosaur. Pelycosaurs were small lizard-like animals that evolved into much larger and very different types.

WOW FACT

Edaphosaurus was a quadruped and was 11 ft (3.2 m) long and weighed about 660 lbs (300 kg).

TEMPERATURE CONTROL

If it got too hot then by standing in a cooling breeze it could cool itself down quickly and effectively.

DID YOU KNOW?

Edaphosaurus is pronounced Ah-daf-oh-saw-us and means 'Earth Lizard' in Greek.

AWESOME

Although Edaphosaurus could chew its food, it also had a very large gut so it would swallow large amounts of partly-chewed leaves and stems. They would ferment in its gut to release the goodness.

TRIASSIC PERIOD

WHEN WAS THE TRIASSIC PERIOD?

The Triassic Period was the first part of the Mesozoic Era, the age of the dinosaurs. It lasted from around 248 to 206 million years ago. During this period, dinosaurs and mammals evolved.

WHAT WAS THE CLIMATE LIKE?

The Triassic climate was generally hot and dry with strong seasons. The formation of the supercontinent of Pangaea at the beginning of the Triassic, 220 million years ago, decreased the amount of shoreline, formed mountains, and gave the interior of the supercontinent a dry, desert-like terrain.

WHAT NO ICE?

The polar regions were moist and temperate and there was no polar ice.

DID YOU KNOW?

The Triassic Period was named in 1834 by the German geologist Friedrich August Von Alberti (1795–1878). It was originally named the 'Trias'.

ANIMALS AND PLANTS IN THE TRIASSIC

There were no dinosaurs at the beginning of the Triassic, but there were many amphibians, some reptiles and dicynodonts. During the early Triassic, corals appeared and ammonites recovered from the Permian extinction. Seed plants dominated the land. 220 million years ago the first mammals appeared. Some scientists believe that mammals evolved from a group of extinct mammal-like reptiles, Theriodontia, which were Therapsids. These primitive mammals were tiny and are thought to have been nocturnal. The very earliest dinosaurs were small, two-legged meat-eaters, such as Coelophysis (see page 44) and Eoraptor (see page 52). The rise of dinosaurs during the late Triassic led to the decline of other previously successful animal groups. Many reptiles and amphibians disappeared and so did advanced mammal-like reptiles.

BIG BANG!

The Triassic period ended with a mass extinction accompanied by huge volcanic eruptions about 208-213 million years ago. Roughly 35% of all animal families died out. Most of the early primitive dinosaurs became extinct, but other more adaptive dinosaurs evolved in the Jurassic. This extinction allowed the dinosaurs to become increasingly dominant, and remained that way for the next 150 million years.

IT'S A MYSTERY!

No one is certain what caused this late Triassic extinction; possibilities include global cooling or an asteroid impact.

DID YOU KNOW?

Turtles, frogs, salamanders, lizards (including snakes), all first appeared in the Triassic.

JURASSIC PERIOD

WHEN WAS THE JURASSIC PERIOD?

After the Triassic Period came the Jurassic Period which lasted from 206 to 144 million years ago. Huge long-necked dinosaurs appeared during the Jurassic era.

DID YOU KNOW?

The Jurassic Period is named after rock strata found in the Jura Mountains, which are located between France and Switzerland.

WHAT WAS THE CLIMATE LIKE?

SUPER FACT

About 140 million years ago, during the late Jurassic period, the flowering plants evolved, and would soon change the face of the Earth.

At the beginning of the Jurassic Period, the climate was hot and dry, but when Pangaea began to break up, there were big flooded areas, tropical forests and coral reefs. The break up of the land and the creation of large seas affected the global climate.

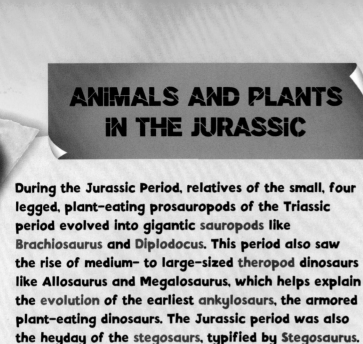

ANIMALS AND PLANTS IN THE JURASSIC

During the Jurassic Period, relatives of the small, four legged, plant-eating prosauropods of the Triassic period evolved into gigantic sauropods like Brachiosaurus and Diplodocus. This period also saw the rise of medium- to large-sized theropod dinosaurs like Allosaurus and Megalosaurus, which helps explain the evolution of the earliest ankylosaurs, the armored plant-eating dinosaurs. The Jurassic period was also the heyday of the stegosaurs, typified by Stegosaurus.

Marine Life Just as dinosaurs grew to bigger and bigger sizes on land, so the marine reptiles of the Jurassic period gradually attained shark-sized proportions. The Jurassic seas were filled with fierce pliosaurs like Liopleurodon, as well as less frightening swimmers like Plesiosaurus. Prehistoric fish were abundant, as were squid and prehistoric sharks, providing a steady source of nourishment for these and other marine reptiles.

Avian Life By the end of the Jurassic period, the skies were filled with relatively advanced pterosaurs like Pteranodon and Dimorphodon.

Plant Life Gigantic herbivorous dinosaurs like Brachiosaurus and Diplodocus couldn't have evolved if they didn't have a reliable source of food: the lands of the Jurassic period had lots of tasty vegetation, including ferns, conifers, cycads, club mosses and horsetails.

SCAN ME
Instructions on page 5

WHAT HAPPENED TO THE JURASSIC?

WOW EVERYWHERE!

There was a minor mass extinction toward the end of the Jurassic period. During this extinction, most of the stegosaurid and enormous sauropod dinosaurs died out, as did many sea creatures. There is some speculation that it was triggered by the release of huge methane deposits from within the Earth. These deposits form beneath the seabed as surface algae dies and sinks to the sea floor.

By the end of the Jurassic Period, dinosaurs had expanded to fill virtually every useable part of the land surface.

CRETACEOUS PERIOD

WHEN WAS THE CRETACEOUS PERIOD?

After the Jurassic Period came the Cretaceous Period lasting from 144 to 65 million years ago. This was the last part of the Mesozoic Era. Most known dinosaurs lived during the Cretaceous period.

DID YOU KNOW?

Creta is the Latin word for chalk. The Cretaceous Period is named after the chalky rock from southeastern England that was the first Cretaceous Period sediment studied.

$$2 + 2 = 4$$

WHAT WAS THE CLIMATE LIKE?

During the early Cretaceous Period, the breakup of the Pangaean supercontinent into smaller continents continued, with the first outlines of modern North and South America, Europe, Asia and Africa taking shape. Conditions were hot and humid like the Jurassic, with the added twist of rising sea levels and the spread of endless swamps, creating an ecological environment in which dinosaurs and other prehistoric life could flourish.

SUPER FACT

Flowers, flowering trees and grasses became more and more common during the Cretaceous period, helped along by the evolution of bees that carried pollen from one flower to another. By the end of the Cretaceous most of the plants on earth were flowering ones.

ANIMALS AND PLANTS IN THE JURASSIC

During the Cretaceous period dinosaurs really came into their own. Thousands of dinosaurs roamed the slowly separating continents, including raptors and tyrannosaurs. There were also other varieties of theropods, including ornithomimids (bird mimics), and lots of small, feathered dinosaurs, including the very intelligent Troodon.

The classic sauropods of the Jurassic Period had pretty much died out, but their descendants, the lightly armored titanosaurs, spread to every continent on earth. Ceratopsians–horned, frilled dinosaurs, like Styracosaurus and Triceratops–became abundant.

Marine Life Shortly after the beginning of the Cretaceous Period, the ichthyosaurs (fish lizards) left the scene, and were replaced by mosasaurs, gigantic pliosaurs like Kronosaurus, and slightly smaller plesiosaurs like Elasmosaurus.

Avian Life By the end of the Cretaceous Period, the pterosaurs (flying reptile), had finally attained the enormous sizes of their cousins on land and in the sea, Quetzalcoathus being a brilliant example. The pterosaurs were gradually crowded out of the sky by the first real prehistoric birds, which evolved from land-dwelling feathered dinosaurs, not pterosaurs.

WOW FACT!

The earliest fossils of birds resembling pelicans, flamingos and sandpipers were from the Cretaceous.

WHAT HAPPENED TO THE CRETACEOUS?

At the end of the Cretaceous Period about 65 million years ago, a mass extinction wiped out the dinosaurs (except for birds) and many other animals. The primary cause of the extinction is thought to be an asteroid impact on the Yucatan Peninsula that raised huge clouds of dust, blotting out the sun and causing most of this vegetation to die out. However there are also lots of other theories for this extinction, including volcanoes and climate change due to continental drift.
The age of reptiles came to an end; the age of mammals was about to begin.

DINOSAUR BRAINS

For a long time palaeontologists have considered dinosaurs to be stupid creatures with small brains and little intelligence. However that view is changing with studies of brains in animals and comparing the intelligence they display alongside the size of their brains.

Intelligence does not always mean you have to have a big brain – the environment you live in plays a part. For example, if all you did all day as a dinosaur was chew plants, then you wouldn't need a big brain to process what you needed to know. However yet you could still be intelligent as all the information you needed to process on a daily basis could be contained within a small brain.

WOW, REALLY?

A stegosaurus would've weighed around three tons and had a brain the same size as a walnut.

ERGH - IS THAT TRUE?

Palaeontologists guess about dinosaur brains from fossils. This is because the brain is an organ and therefore one of the first parts to rot away (decompose) when the dinosaur dies.

BRAIN STATS

	10%	20%	30%	40%

A human brain weight is 2.5% of the overall body weight — 2.5%

A rat's brain is 0.85% — 0.85%

A dog's brain is 2.5% — 2.5%

A sparrow's brain is 4.2% — 4.2%

A Diplodocus brain is 0.001% — 0.001%

AND THE WINNER IS...

Troodon, a member of the Theropoda from the Cretaceous period. The Troodon was the same height as a human, had large eyes positioned to give it stereo vision and, due to it being a biped with long hind legs, it was very fast.

Palaeontologists believe that Troodon had a 'big' brain (about the size of an Ostrich) and when brain size compared to its body weight as per other dinosaurs was way ahead.

DID YOU KNOW?

Troodon means 'wounding tooth' and it got this name from the sharp serrated tooth it had for ripping up meat and flesh.

HEADS AND TAILS

Every dinosaur was made up of the same skeleton, but basic body parts, like heads and tails, had different appearances and functions. Sizes of heads and tails varied greatly across the various species of dinosaur.

Studies of dinosaurs' skulls in particular has given scientists lots of important information about their lifestyle and intelligence.

HEAD FACTS

The biggest dinosaurs often had very small heads. A 30 ton Brachiosaurus may have eaten up to a ton of plants every day just to stay alive. However it had a head not much larger than a horse and teeth that couldn't chew!

NUMB SKULL

Dinosaur skulls differed from dinosaur to dinosaur depending on what it was needed for. Deinonychus (see page 36) had a lightweight skull, while T-Rex (see page 30) had a large head which was heavily reinforced with bone and shock-absorbing muscle to withstand the impact of crashing into its victims.

Q: Which dinosaur had the biggest head?

A: Torosaurus, a horned dinosaur related to triceratops. It had a skull 8 feet (or 2.4m) long, longer than any animal on land ever!

TAIL FACTS

Like heads, dinosaurs' tails varied according to use. Ankylosaurus (see page 110) had a heavily armored tail. Ankylosaurus, if attacked, could use its club-like tail as a weapon, swinging it from side to side like a knight's mace.

IT WASN'T ALWAYS EASY!

Scientists occasionally got it wrong, here are two famous mix ups.

THE ELASMOSAURUS WITH ITS HEAD ON ITS TAIL

In 1868, paleontologist Edward Drinker Cope reconstructed an Elasmosaurus skeleton with its head on its tail. The error was quickly pointed out in a very unfriendly manner by Cope's rival, Othniel C Marsh and the dispute escalated into what we now know as the 'Bone War'.

THE STEGOSAURUS WITH A BRAIN IN ITS BOTTOM!

However Othniel Marsh made a mistake of his own. When Stegosaurus was first discovered, in 1877, he mooted the idea that it had a second brain in its bottom. Today, it is believed that Stegosaurus did not have two brains, and the cavity in this stegosaur's tail was used to store extra food.

SENSES

It is hard to tell what dinosaurs were like because we have never been able to watch them and observe how they behave. Scientists, however, can work out information about their senses from evidence left behind. Like all living things, dinosaurs had five senses; taste, touch, sight, sound and smell.

TASTE FACTS

A dinosaur's sense of taste would have been much more developed than its touch. Plant-eating dinosaurs would have used taste to tell the difference between certain foods. However some scientists now believe that plant-eaters may not have had a very good sense of taste after all, like modern day reptiles who don't have much of a sense of taste. It is thought they would not have been able to taste bitter and poisonous alkaloids contained in some flowering plants evolving in the Late Cretaceous Period, and this may be one of the reasons they died out.

DEADLEY

SIGHT FACTS

Most dinosaurs would have had good side vision, with eyes set at the sides of their heads, but because their eyes didn't face forward, they weren't very good at judging distance.
Troodon (see page 56) had exceptionally large eyes, based on the size of the eye sockets, and would have had very good vision.
Opthalmosaurus had massive eyes which would have helped it see in the dark deep oceans – large eyes can house more light-gathering cells and so are more effective in the dark.

SOUND FACTS

Dinosaurs did not have exterior ear flaps like mammals but heard through holes set far back in the head behind their eyes. It was probably herding dinosaurs, with their strong need to communicate, that had the most acute sense of hearing.
Hadrosaurs (see page 80) display the only real evidence so far of being able to make noises, with a variety of nasal trumpets and air sacs.
It is likely dinosaurs would probably have made noises, if they needed to.

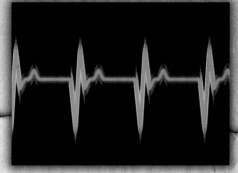

TOUCH FACTS

A dinosaur's sense of touch was probably not very well developed, because of their thick skin. However there is some evidence to suggest Velociraptor's (see page 50) nose was very sensitive to touch!

SMELL FACTS

The meat-eating predators were probably able to smell very well, in order to hunt their prey. This evidence is based on the size and shape of their olfactory lobes (the parts of the brain linked to smell). Tyrannosaurus Rex (see page 30) and Giganotosaurus (see page 32), the largest meat-eaters of all time, had a keen sense of smell and good eyesight. They could pick up the scent of dead bodies from a long distance, from which they could scavenge meat.

MEAT-EATERS

In the next few pages you will find some of the most famous and frightening meat-eating dinosaurs that roamed our planet during the Triassic, Jurassic and Cretaceous Periods.

INTRODUCING ...

TYRANNOSAURUS REX

GIGANOTOSAURUS

HERRERASAURUS

DEINONYCHUS

PROCOMPSOGNATHUS

BARYONYX

CARCHARODONTOSAURUS

COMPSOGNATHUS

COELOPHYSIS

DROMAEOSAURUS

COELURUS

VELOCIRAPTOR

EORAPTOR

OVIRAPTOR
PHILOCERATOPS

TROODON

ACROCANTHOSAURUS

MEGALOSAURUS

ALLOSAURUS

SPINOSAURUS

CARNOTAURUS

SAURORNITHOIDES

TYRANNOSAURUS REX

King of the dinosaurs, the Tyrannosaurus Rex is probably the best-known dinosaur. It is also one of the largest carnivores ever discovered. It lived during the last days of the Cretaceous Period.

SCAN ME
Instructions on page 5

T-REX STATS AND FACTS

NAME:	Tyrannosaurus
HEIGHT:	23 ft (7 m)
LENGTH:	up to 39 ft (12 m)
SPECIAL FEATURES:	Sharp teeth, each measuring 7-12 in (18-30 cm) long
DIET:	Meat – almost any other animal
LIVED:	70-65 Million Years Ago
FOSSILS FOUND:	Canada and the USA

DID YOU KNOW?

Although Tyrannosaurus is often pictured as being green, no-one actually knows if it was. Fossils don't give us any clues, so scientists look at modern-day animals such as crocodiles and lizards to help them guess what a dinosaur's scaly skin might have looked like.

WOW, AMAZING

Some experts think that Tyrannosaurus might have been a scavenger, rather than a hunter. Other scientists disagree, and it is one of the longest-running arguments in paleontology. Instead of hunting and killing prey themselves, scavengers find and eat animals that are already dead.

AWESOME FACT!

Tyrannosaurus' teeth were fixed into its gums, rather than its jawbone. This allowed new rows of teeth to grow underneath. When a tooth was lost, broken, or old, it fell out, and a sharp new one took its place.

GiGANOTOSAURUS

Giganotosaurus means 'Giant Southern Lizard' and they lived at the same time as enormous plant-eating dinosaurs like the Argentinosaurus, which it hunted. A dominant predator, it is the largest known meat-eater, even bigger than T-Rex!

From its skull, which was over 6 ft or 1.8 m, we know that it probably had a good sense of smell and excellent eyesight thanks to its large eyes.

WHAT A WHOPPER!

Giganotosaurus weighed as much as 125 people. It also hunted prey up to 10 times its own size.

NO WAY

The biggest Giganotosaurus found was over a metre longer and a ton heavier than 'Sue' the largest known T-Rex. Not to be confused with... Another dinosaur called Gigantosaurus (different spelling) which is an African sauropod (giant long necked dinosaurs like the diplodocus).

GIGANOTOSAURUS STATS

NAME: Giganotosaurus

DESCRIPTION: Large powerful carnivore

NOTE: This is not the same dinosaur as the African sauropod Gigantosaurus (different spelling!) named by Seeley in 1869.

HEIGHT: 18ft (5.5m)

LENGTH: 49ft (15m)

SKULL SIZE: 6ft (1.8m)

FOUND: In various sites in South America, mainly Argentina. It hunted in warm, swampy areas like its famous cousin Tyrannosaurus Rex.

WATCH THOSE FINGERS!

Giganotosaurus did not have the crushing bite of T-Rex, and so would have attacked by slashing its victims with its three clawed fingers.

BANANA BRAIN

Giganotosaurus had a brain the shape and size of a banana! Even though it had a skull the size of a bathtub.

IT'S A GIANT

Look how the Giganotosaurus compares to other dinosaurs, pictured are (from small to large) the Compsognathus, Ornitholestes, Dilophosaurus, Torosaurus, Giganotosaurus and the Camarasaurus.

39

HERRERASAURUS

Herrerasaurus was named after a rancher called Victorino Herrera. He found Herrerasaurus fossils in rocks in the foothills of the Andes mountain range in Argentina. Herrerasaurus was one of the earliest dinosaurs and lived during the Triassic Period.

Despite its small size Herrerasaurus was an active and very dangerous predator, it would have been a fast bipedal runner and taken advantage of sharp teeth, and three-fingered hands to capture prey.

NATURAL HUNTER

With its strong hind legs, short thighs and long feet it was a natural hunter. Fast and agile it would hunt down its prey of small and medium-sized dinosaurs and feast on them with its large jaw and sharp teeth to tear and chew on the meat.

DISCOVERY FACT

The first skull of the Herrerasaurus was not found until 1988. This discovery, along with an almost complete skeleton, finally allowed palaeontologists to classify the dinosaur as a Theropod.

HERRERASAURUS STATS

NAME:	Herrerasaurus
HEIGHT:	3.3 ft (1.1 m)
LENGTH:	10-20 ft (3-6 m)
SPECIAL FEATURES:	Strong hind legs, fast runner, sharp backward facing teeth to grip prey.

WOW

Herrerasaurus was about the same length as the Komodo dragon, a giant lizard that lives today in Indonesia.

DEINONYCHUS

The name Deinonychus means 'terrible claw'. It was a carnivorous dinosaur and was bipedal. It lived in the forests of North America in the middle Cretaceous Period around 100 million years ago. Deinonychus was about 4 ft or 1.5 m tall, weighed about 176 lb or 80 kg and measured 10 ft or 3 m from the tip of its nose to the end of its long, rigid tail. It had a large head with powerful jaws and sharp serrated teeth. Large eye sockets indicate it probably also had excellent eyesight.

DEADLY!

Fossil evidence shows Deinonychus packs hunted and killed Tenontosaurus, a dinosaur ten times their size.

SCAN ME
Instructions on page 5

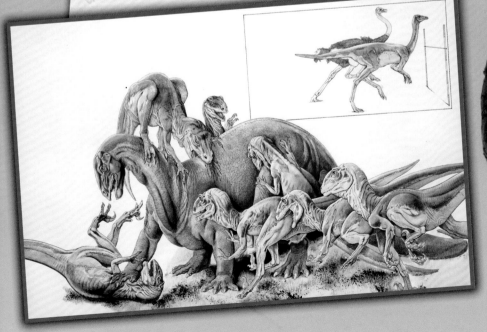

GORY!

Deinonychus' likely method of attack was to use its powerful back legs to leap into the air and land on its prey, kicking the long sickle toe-claws in, causing significant damage and anchoring it firmly. It would tear and bite at prey to cause as much blood loss as possible.

MILITARY PRECISION!

The dromaeosauridae family all have quite large brains in comparison to their total body size, meaning they were some of the brightest dinosaurs around. This would have allowed them to work together as a team and use simple tactics to guide their prey towards other members of the pack.

TERRIBLE CLAW

Deinonychus' second toe sported a vicious 5 in or 13 cm long claw which is how it got its name. This claw could be held up out of the way whilst the creature was running, only snapping into position when needed for the attack. It was originally thought its long claw was used to slash prey but recent tests have shown that it was more likely used as a stabbing weapon like a knife.

PROCOMPSOGNATHUS

Procompsognathus means 'before the elegant jaw'. It lived during the late Triassic around 210 million years ago, in the swamps of Western Europe. It was fast on its feet and caught insects, lizards, bugs and newly-hatched reptiles to eat, chewing them up with its many small teeth. Procompsognathus walked upright on its long hind legs, balancing with its long stiff pointed tail which it held off the ground. Its arms were short with large four-fingered clawed hands which it would have used for grabbing its prey.

NASTY!

It is believed that Procompsognathus could inflict a poisonous bite although this has not been proved.

STILL A LOT TO FIND OUT

The poor quality of its fossil remains means we still do not know much about Procompsognathus. However this small dinosaur was the base of the evolution of the very sucessful family called Theropoda.

WOW FACT!

Procompsognathus was about the same weight as a pet cat– 4–7 lbs (1.8–3.2kg), although it was 4 ft or 1.3 m long. It was one of the tiniest dinosaurs, and also one of the earliest.

FOSSIL FACT!

Procompsognathus fossils have been discovered in Wittenberge, Germany. It was discovered by Eberhard Fraas in 1913.

BARYONYX

From the early Cretaceous Period this meat-eating dinosaur was the biggest in Europe. It lived in southern England near modern-day Southampton and Portsmouth. There is a skeleton of this English dinosaur in the Natural History Museum in London after its discovery in a clay pit in 1983 by William Walker, an amateur fossil collector.

HOW DO YOU SAY MY NAME?

Bar-ee-on-iks

FISHY BUSINESS

This dinosaur was one of the few confirmed piscivorous (fish-eating) dinosaurs as fish scales were found in the stomach of its fossil.
Scientists believe that Baryonyx would have waited on the banks or in shallow waters for fish to move past and may have used its large claws to scoop them out of the water. It would have been able to hold its head underwater, as its nostrils were high enough up on its skull for it to have its jaws underwater and still be able to breathe.

DID YOU KNOW?

The shape and size of Baryonyx's back legs suggest it would have been a fast runner.

CROCO-DINO-SAUR?

Very much like our modern-day crocodiles this dinosaur had many teeth packed into its long jaw. It had twice as many as the Tyranosaurus Rex.

It also had crocodile-like adaptations, such as a sharp angle on the upper jaw near the snout to prevent fish escaping.

THUMB FACTS

BARYONYX:	means 'Heavy Claw'
CLASSIFICATION:	Theropoda, Spinosauridae
ATE:	Fish and scavenged
LENGTH:	33 ft (10 m)
HEIGHT:	8 ft 9 in (2.65 m)
WEIGHT:	5290 lb (2400 kg)
FEATURES:	Long crocodile-like jaw, large claw (10 in or 25 cm) on thumb of each hand

CARCHARODONTOSAURUS

Nearly as large as the Tyrannosaurus Rex, this large meat-eater lived in modern-day North Africa 105 to 94 million years ago. The environment was very different there at that time with many rivers and lakes flowing through rainforests and was very hot and humid.

ENVIRONMENT CHANGE

The environment is always changing due to many factors including the sun, volcanoes and movements of the continents. North Africa is now dry and barren with many large sandy desserts. When the Carcharodontosaurus lived there, it was wet and hot with lots of plants, forests and animals which made it good hunting grounds.

EWW GROSS!

Whilst Carcharodontosaurus may have used his enormous jaw and many long serrated teeth to hunt its prey it would have also scavenged, eating rotting carcasses of dead animals – it must have had very smelly breath!

CASUALTY OF WAR

Carcharodontosaurus fossils were first discovered by Charles Deperet and J. Savornin in North Africa in 1927. Unfortunately the first fossils were destroyed during World War II. Luckily further fossils were subsequently found in North Africa by paleontologist Paul Sereno in 1996.

LONG IN THE TOOTH NAME

Its long name is almost as long as its 8 inch (20cm) teeth and one of the largest ever Therapod skulls found is 5 ft (1.6 m) long. However the Giganotosaurus had the biggest skull.

COMPSOGNATHUS

Compsognathus was one of the first complete dinosaur skeletons ever found. It is also one of the smallest, with a body about the size of a chicken and a head to tail length of around 3.8 ft or 1 m. It lived in modern-day France and Germany during the late Jurassic Period in a tropical environment.

Compsognathus was an early member of a group of dinosaurs called the coelurosaurs (hollow-tail lizards). Later members of the coelurosaur group included the most likely ancestors of birds.

YOU'LL NEVER GUESS WHAT

At the time of this dinosaur Europe was an Archipelago, a series of tropical islands in the sea, like modern day Indonesia. Anyone for a coconut?

SMALL BUT DEADLY

This dinosaur may have been small but it was fast, agile and had very sharp teeth. The first fossil found in Germany had the remains of a lizard in its stomach cavity, its last meal before death. Have you ever tried to catch a lizard? Think of how fast you would have to be!

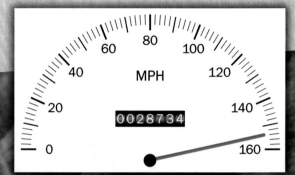

0028734

MOVIE STAR

Compsognathus featured throughout the dinosaur movie The Lost World: Jurassic Park where it hunted in large packs overwhelming much larger prey than itself.

HOW MANY FINGERS?

Paleontologists cannot agree over whether Compsognathus had two or three fingers on each hand. Either way, those slender fingers would have helped with grasping prey, which could then be swallowed whole or torn into pieces by tiny, sharp teeth.

COELOPHYSIS

Coelophysis lived during the late Triassic period, roughly 210 million years ago and is one of the earliest-known dinosaurs. Coelophysis was a meat-eater and may have also been a cannibal. They moved around on hind legs, in an upright position. Coelophysis lived in what was then a desert-like environment, perhaps like modern-day Kenya without the grasses.

Coelophysis probably moved around in packs and hunted together. Their teeth were like blades with fine serrations like a knife, which suggests that they were predatory dinosaurs.

AWESOME

An interesting fact of the Coelophysis is that it had a wish bone, just like a chicken, which is the earliest example known in a dinosaur.

DID YOU KNOW?

Coelophysis, pronounced See-law-fys-iss means 'hollow form', because Coelophysis had hollow bones, so their bodies were very light.

COELOPHYSIS THE CANNIBAL

Some scientists believe that Coelophysis were cannibals, as one fossil found had a baby Coelophysis in its stomach.

TO INFINITY AND BEYOND!

Coelophysis has actually journeyed into space. Its skull was taken aboard the space shuttle Endeavor mission STS-89 in 1988.

AWESOME TAIL

Coelophysis used its tail like a rudder when it was moving, so that it could keep its balance.

53

DROMAEOSAURUS

Dromaeosaurus was the first to be discovered of a group of infamous dinosaurs nicknamed the 'raptors'. It lived in and around North Western America and Canada during the late Cretaceous Period. Dromaeosaurus means 'fast running lizard' however this whole group of dinosaurs, Dromaeosurids (raptors), are believed to be the most closely related to birds.

PACK HUNTERS

Dromaeosaurus teeth have been found among the fossils of much larger dinosaurs suggesting they hunted in packs like wolves so that they could bring down much larger prey.

I BELIEVE I CAN FLY

Unfortunately not, however some believe their descendants flew and became used to ground dwelling so they became bigger and stopped flying, like modern day ostriches and emus. Also some Paleontologists have suggested that these dinosaurs may have had colorful feathers head to toe!

MINI-TYRANNOSAURUS?

With its deep, large jaw, short and massive skull as well as big strong teeth, Dromaeosaurus looks like a mini version of the Tyrannosaurs.

DEADLY WEAPONS

The Dromaesaurus had an arsenal of weapons and skills at its disposal:
- Sickle shaped killing claw on the hind feet used for disembowelling prey. Its size was about 6 ft (1.8 m), large enough to pack a punch if it jumped onto its prey.
- It had very large eyes providing excellent vision and hunting prowess.
- Many sharp and strong teeth in a long jaw meant it could not only tear the meat of its prey but hang on and grapple them to the ground.
- Powerful hind legs allowed it to run at very fast speeds and jump high.
- A stiff and straight tail allowed it to balance while hunting prey meaning it could be very agile across all sorts of terrain.

COELURUS

Theropods are often thought of as large, fierce animals but many were often small. Just like we have big predators like tigers and wolves in the modern world, we also have smaller killers like weasals and foxes. This is the same in the dinosaur age with dinosaurs like the Coelurus being a well-adapted small predator. It lived in Central and Western USA, during the Jurassic Period and hunted around swampy areas eating frogs, lizards and insects.

WHO FOUND COELURUS

Coelurus was discovered by the famous dinosaur hunter Othniel Marsh in 1879 at the Morrison Formation rocks in Wyoming, USA.

COULD THIS BE TRUE?

Recent studies have concluded in the U.S.A. that foxes may well have in-built 'augmented reality' and use the Earth's magnetic fields to judge distance as well as direction - Could Coelurus have had this skill as well?

FACT BOX

Weasels hunt mainly by scent and although small investigates every small hole and crevice it comes across until it can find its prey and kill it with a short sharp bite to the neck. Paleontologists believe that this deadly way of killing was likely the preferred method for Coelurus.

BONE WARS : OTHNIEL CHARLES MARSH (1831-1899)

Othniel Marsh was a famous American dinosaur hunter and is responsible for the discovery of many of the dinosaurs we know today.

Allosaurus (1877), Ammosaurus (1890), Anchisaurus (1885), Apatosaurus (1877), Atlantosaurus (1877), Barosaurus (1890), Camptosaurus (1885), Ceratops (1888), Ceratosaurus (1884), Claosaurus (1890), Coelurus (1879), Creosaurus (1878), Diplodocus (1878), Diracodon (1881), Dryosaurus (1894), Dryptosaurus (1877), Labrosaurus (1896), Laosaurus (1878), Nanosaurus (1877), Nodosaurus (1889), Ornithomimus (1890), Pleurocoelus (1891), Priconodon (1888), Stegosaurus (1877), Torosaurus (1891), Triceratops (1889)

Marsh also competed against a fellow Palaeontologist called Edward Cope in the "Bone Wars". They were both very competitive and between them discovered over 120 new species of dinosaur. Marsh triumphed in the Bone Wars by discovering 80 new species compared with Cope's meagre 56. Cope did not like this and they continued arguing in scientific journals for many years to come.

COELURUS FACT-FILE

PRONOUNCIATION:	cee–loor–uss
MEAT EATER:	Frogs, Lizards, Large Insects
SIZE:	6 ft (2 m) long
WEIGHT:	15 kg (33 lb)
DESCRIPTION:	Small, low head 8 in long (20 cm)
	Long and flexible neck
	Very long and slim tail
	Strong long thighs, walked upright
	Hollow tail bones

57

VELOCIRAPTOR

The Velociraptor is probably the best known of the Dromaeosaurids and one of the most infamous dinosaurs that lived during the late Cretaceous period around 70 million years ago. Velocirpator means 'speedy thief' and would have hunted viciously in a desert-like environment around modern day China, Mongolia and Central Russia.

BEWARE OF THE BIRDS!

Some scientists belief that the Velocirapator was very closely related to birds and may have been slightly warm blooded with a covering of feathers. Scientists also believe that they may have been able to breathe in a special way, like birds, and keep pockets of air in their hollow bones. This would enable very fast acceleration and high speeds of up to 60 kph (37 mph).

TOP TRUMP FACTS

SIZE: 5-6 ft (1.5-2 m) and stood on two legs

SPEED: 60 kph (37 mph)

JUMP: 12 ft (3.6 m)

INTELLIGENCE: One of the most intelligent of all the dinosaurs

VISION: Large eyes gave it excellent hunter vision even in the dark

WEAPONS: Deadly sickle like claws on hind feet to grab and slash at prey. 80 sharp bladed teeth some 1 in (2.5 cm) long

WHO'S A CLEVER DINO...

In comparison to its body size the velociraptor had an enormous brain for that of a dinosaur. This probably meant it was very clever and could problem solve. It also meant that they were probably social and hunted in packs to great effect.

MOVIE STAR

The velociraptors featured heavily throughout the dinosaur movie Jurassic Park where it used its intelligence to hunt down the main human characters.

JURASSIC PARK

EORAPTOR

Eoraptor is one of the earliest known dinosaurs and lived 228 million years ago during the late Triassic Period. It ate other reptiles and small herbivorous dinosaurs and its fossils have been found in the foothills of the Andes in South America.

GREEDY DINO

Eoraptor was probably an omnivore which means it would have eaten plants and vegetation as well as other small reptiles and herbivorous dinosaurs.

IT'S A SMALL ONE!

The Eoraptor was no taller than a small child.

SMELLY BREATH

Like that of the modern-day Komodo dragon, the Eoraptor probably had very smelly breath and bacterial teeth as its front teeth were leaf-shaped, meaning it needed to eat soft food such as rotting carcasses of dead dinosaurs.

EORAPTOR FACT-FILE

PRONUNCIATION:	EE – OH – RAP – TOR
MEAT EATER AND SCAVENGER:	Frogs, Lizards, Large Insects
LENGTH:	3 ft (1 m) long
WEIGHT:	6 – 33 lb (3 – 15 kg)
SPECIAL FEATURES:	Light body, quick and agile
	Long legs, walked upright
	Hollow tail bones

DID YOU KNOW?

Eoraptor also had arms, which were only half the length of its legs. It had sharp claws on each hand that would have been used to catch and tear its prey.

OVIRAPTOR PHILOCERATOPS

The first Oviraptor Philoceratops fossils were discovered in the Gobi desert, Mongolia in 1914. This strange bird-looking dinosaur lived in the late Cretaceous Period around 75 million years ago.

Fossilized dinosaur egg

OMNIVORE

Omnivore dinosaurs are quite rare as most were either Carnivores (meat eating) or Herbivores (plant eating) exclusively. Omnivores will eat anything they can find and the Oviraptor's funny shaped beak jaw was well equipped to deal with a variety of food from shellfish, scavenged meat, insects and eggs to plants.

SPEEDY BIRDOSAURUS

Did you know that the Oviraptor could run 43 mph (70 km/h).

IT WASN'T ME OFFICER ... HONEST!

The Oviraptor Philoceratops was thought to be an egg-stealing dinosaur as the first fossilized skull of this dinosaur was found 4 inches (10cm) away from an egg believed to be that of a Ceratops. Oviraptor means egg thief and Philoceratops means 'like Ceratops'. However a later discovery shows that the egg was that of the Oviraptor and it was tending to its eggs rather than trying to eat them.

WOW

Recent finds have concluded that not all dinosaur feathers were for flight or for keeping warm. Two 125 million old fossils found in China in 2009 show early feather formations, previously unknown to Science.

DINO FACTS

PRONUNCIATION:	O – VIH – RAP – TOR
OMNIVORE:	Frogs, Lizards, Large Insects, Plants,
LENGTH:	6 - 8 ft (1.8 – 2.5 m) long
WEIGHT:	80 lb (36 kg)
SPECIAL FEATURES:	Horny crest on head for mating displays
	Toothless beak
	Bird-like in many ways, it may have been covered in feathers
	May have sat on eggs so probably warm-blooded

TROODON

Troodon was one of the first ever dinosaurs discovered in North America, in 1855. Troodon means 'wounding tooth' named after the serrated tooth that was the first part of the skeleton to be found. They lived all over what is modern-day Western USA and further north to Canada during the late Cretaceous period.

NEST SWEET NEST

Like the Oviraptor Philoceratops and ground-dwelling birds, Troodon would make a nest on the ground and brood over its eggs like a hen.

FUSSY EATER?

Troodon's teeth were not like the teeth of typical meat-eaters. They had little serrations running up and down the back of the teeth like most meat-eaters but there were also larger bumps along the side like plant-eating dinosaurs. This has led some to believe that Troodon was not a fussy eater and may have eaten insects, eggs and even plants as well as small animals, lizards and baby dinosaurs. This would make Troodon one of the rare Omnivore dinosaurs.

THUMBS UP FOR INTELLIGENCE

Scientist believe that having opposable thumbs (hands that are mirror images of each other rather than identical) has been a critical factor in human evolution. Troodons also had opposable thumbs as well as a large brain (in comparison to body size). This means that as one of the cleverest dinosaurs they may have evolved into even more intelligent animals, had they not become extinct.

NIGHT STALKER

Troodons had large, slightly forward facing eyes which gave them incredible eyesight and a good sense of distance (binocular vision). They would have used these eyes to their advantage when hunting at dusk or twilight.

ROBO-SAURUS

MIT university has built 'Troody' a robotic version of a Troodon to see how the 12 ft (3.5 m) long 3 ft (1 m) tall dinosaur would have walked.

ACROCANTHOSAURUS

Acrocanthosaurus means 'high-spined lizard' it lived in the early Cretaceous Period, roughly 115–105 million years ago, in the tropics near sea level. Its name came from the unusual spikes which grew out of its spine. 'Acro' as the dinosaur is often nicknamed was 42 ft or 13 m long and weighed 5,000 lbs or 2300 kg. It was a meat-eater and was a large, fierce predator that could kill even large sauropods. Acro is thought to have been a scavenger too. Its teeth were designed for tearing meat from the bones of its prey.

STRONGER THAN YOU THINK!

This dinosaur would probably be able to lift a small car off the ground if it were alive today. Its arms were larger and more powerful than those of T-rex itself.

LIKE A SHARK!

As any of its 68 serrated teeth broke, another was ready to take its place. Like a shark, Acro was constantly shedding old teeth and replacing them with new ones.

HOW MUCH?

In 1998, the fossil skeleton of an Acrocanthosaurus nicknamed 'Fran' was bought for the North Carolina Museum of Natural Sciences for '3 milion, believed to be the second highest price ever paid for a dinosaur.

DID YOU KNOW?

In 2005, scientists constructed a replica of Acro's brain, using CT scanning technology on a fossil skull. The result showed that the brain was more like that of a crocodile than a bird in shape and that Acro had excellent hearing, its head would have been held at an angle.

MEGALOSAURUS

Megalosaurus means 'Great Lizard' it was found in the forests of Western Europe during the late Jurassic Period around 160 million years ago. This carnivore grew to a length of 30 ft or 9 m and weighed about a ton. It walked on two legs and had a long tail to help balance out its heavy head. Megalosaurus was a powerful hunter and could even attack the largest prey. It probably also scavenged from dead bodies as part of its diet. Its back legs were much longer than its arms and these arms had hands that could have been used for grasping. The legs would have ended in four-toed feet, which had strong, sharp claws.

Fossils have been found in Europe, Asia, Africa and South America

A GIANT MAN?

Megalosaurus was named in 1824 and was the first dinosaur to be named. In 1676 a fossilized femur of Megalosaurus was dug up in England, and it was declared to be a giant man! It wasn't until 150 years later that it was given its name, by palaeontologist William Buckland.

WALKED LIKE A DUCK

Megalosaurus waddled rather like a duck, its tail swishing from side to side! Scientists have studied its fossilized footprints which showed that its feet pointed inwards as it walked.

STATS

PRONUNCIATION:	meg-uh-low-sawr-ussu
BORDER:	Therapoda
FAMILY:	Megalosauridae
DESCRIPTION:	large bipedal carnivore
FEATURES:	powerful jaws, bulky body, large head
DIET:	other dinosaurs

DID YOU KNOW?

Scientists estimated that Megalosaurus could run at around 18 miles per hour or 29 km/ph. Although it would usually have plodded along at around 4 miles per hour or 7 km/ph.

ALLOSAURUS

Allosaurus means 'different lizard', and was the most common large predator in North America during the Jurassic Period around 155–145 million years ago. It was between 23–29 ft (7–9 m) in length, and weighed between 1–4 tons. It had a huge head, long strong hind legs and very powerful arms. It also had very large claws on its hands. Allosaurus' jaws were able to expand to allow larger chunks of food to be swallowed. Footprint evidence suggests that Allosaurus hunted in packs and may have raised its young in large nests.

SCAN ME
Instructions on page 5

WOW SPEEDY

Allosaurus was light thanks to the clever air sacs in its bones. It would have been able to run at almost 37 miles per hour (60 kmh).

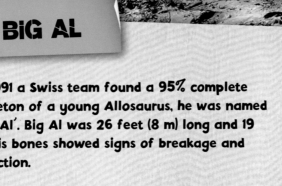

BIG AL

In 1991 a Swiss team found a 95% complete skeleton of a young Allosaurus, he was named 'Big Al'. Big Al was 26 feet (8 m) long and 19 of his bones showed signs of breakage and infection.

LIKE AN AX

Allosaurus' skull was very light, but capable of withstanding massive upward forces. It attacked its prey by opening its mouth wide and using powerful neck muscles to drive its upper jaw downwards, slamming into its prey like an ax, tearing away hunks of flesh.

FOSSIL FACT

Fossils have been found in the Western USA and Europe. The first specimen was named by Othniel C Marsh in 1877.

DID YOU KNOW?

Scientists at Cambridge University (England) recently created a 3D computer model of 'Big Al' and by using engineering techniques they were able to calculate that the jaws would have had a very weak bite, and would have struggled to break the skulls of most large living creatures.

SPINOSAURUS

Spinosaurus means 'spined lizard' after the row of high spines running down its backbone, which probably had skin stretched between them to form a 'sail' up to 6 ft or 2 m tall, taller than any other dinosaur. This enormous dinosaur lived in the late Cretaceous Period, around 98 to 95 million years ago, in what is now called Africa. Spinosaurus walked on two legs, and had a long slender nose with jaws resembling a crocodile. Its teeth were not sharp flesh ripping scythes like Gigantosaurus, but long, conical and interlocked suggesting their main diet was probably fish.

MOVIE STAR

Spinosaurus is the main villain of *Jurassic Park III*, in which it battles a T-Rex and comes out the winner.

JURASSIC PARK

BIG HEAD!

Spinosaurus had a skull, 5 ft 9 in or 1.75 m long. That's as long as a tall human!

WOW MASSIVE

In February 2006 it was revealed that Spinosaurus was the biggest meat-eating dinosaur of all, even bigger than T-rex. It measured 56 ft or 17 m long and would have weighed 7–9 tons.

FOSSIL FACTS

Spinosaurus was discovered by German geologist and palaeontologist Ernst Stromer in 1911 in Egypt.

CARNOTAURUS

Carnotaurus means 'meat-eating bull' it was another enormous dinosaur that lived during the Cretaceous Period around 113 to 91 million years ago in what is now Argentina. It had a small skull, a broad chest and a thin tail and had unusually small arms. Carnotaurus was bipedal and grew to about 25 ft or 7.6 m long and stood about 15 ft or 4.6 m high. We do not know if it had the speed and agility to hunt down prey, but its short pointed teeth show us it was a meat-eater. Instead of hunting, it may have scavenged from the bodies of dead animals.

HORNS OF A BULL

Carnotaurus was named in 1985 by José F Bonaparte after its most notable feature – the two horns located above its eyes, resembling those of a bull. The first and only fossil was found in Patagonia, South America.

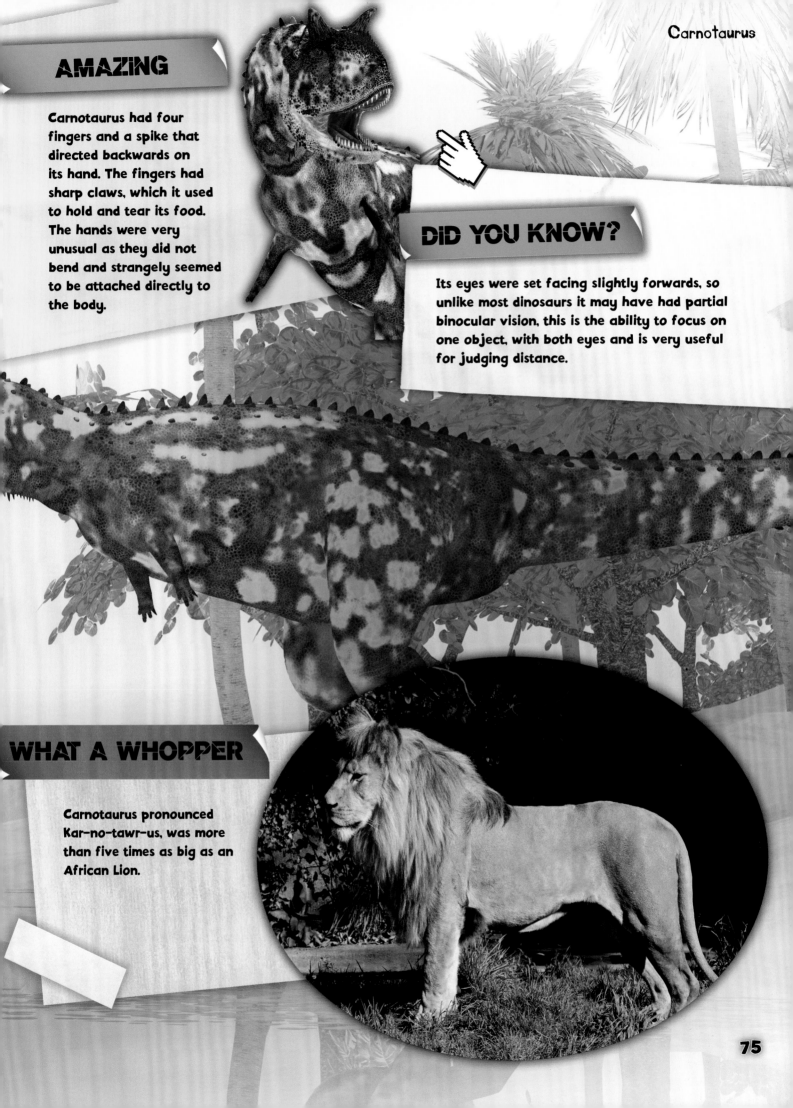

AMAZING

Carnotaurus had four fingers and a spike that directed backwards on its hand. The fingers had sharp claws, which it used to hold and tear its food. The hands were very unusual as they did not bend and strangely seemed to be attached directly to the body.

DID YOU KNOW?

Its eyes were set facing slightly forwards, so unlike most dinosaurs it may have had partial binocular vision, this is the ability to focus on one object, with both eyes and is very useful for judging distance.

WHAT A WHOPPER

Carnotaurus pronounced Kar-no-tawr-us, was more than five times as big as an African Lion.

SAURORNITHOIDES

Saurornithoides means 'bird-like lizard' and it was a highly-efficient predator that roamed the plains of central Asia during the Cretaceous Period around 70–65 million years ago. It had a long, low head and sharp, closely-packed teeth and would have been between 6–10 ft or 2–3 m in length and weighed about 29–59 lbs or 13–27 kg. Like other raptors, it ran on its strong hind legs and probably used its long arms and grasping hands to seize and tear live prey, including small mammals and possibly other dinosaur hatchlings.

at

AWESOME EYES

It was sharp-eyed as it had large eyes and binocular vision. It also would have had excellent night vision and some scientists believe it may have been primarily nocturnal when hunting for prey.

DID YOU KNOW?

Saurornithoides had an especially long, vicious claw on its hind feet, which was attached to the fourth toe, and was retractable when running or walking.

FOSSIL FACTS

Fossils have been found in Mongolia. The first fossil was found in the 1920s by an expedition led by Roy Chapman Andrews.

IS IT A BIRD?

When the fossils of Saurornithoides were first found it fooled paleontologists because it had a long narrow snout they thought it was an ancient bird.
Scientists now think that maybe it wasn't 'lizard-like' and perhaps rather than skin, it could've been covered in feathers.

WHO'S A CLEVER DINO!

Saurornithoides had a very large brain compared to the size of its body, making it one of the most intelligent of the dinosaurs. Its brain was six times as big of that of a crocodile.

77

COLOR AND CAMOUFLAGE

No one knows for sure what color dinosaurs actually were, although they are often shown as green or brown. This is because animal's skin color is produced by organic pigments which are not preserved when fossils are formed. Scientists do know however, that dinosaurs were covered with tough, scaly skin like modern reptiles. While large meat-eaters and armored dinosaurs may not have needed color or camouflage, the smaller ones would of needed this kind of defense to hide from predators.

AWESOME!

It is likely that color would of been used by dinosaurs to find a mate. Much like animals today, color announces the male is ready to breed and helps females with a choice of mate.

COOL FACT!

Stegosaurus had two rows of diamond-shaped plates along its back and each of these plates were filled with tiny blood vessels. If Stegosaurus needed to cool down blood was pumped into these plates which would have turned them bright red.

DID YOU KNOW?

Bright colors in nature normally mean a poisonous species. Big animals don't usually have bright colors.

CAMOUFLAGE FACT

Like modern animals today, dinosaurs probably used color to conceal, disguise and identify themselves. Dinosaurs more than likely had pale undersides to reduce shadows, and striped or spotted patterns to help them blend in amongst the plants and vegetation.

WOW FACT!

A recent discovery of a mummified Hadrosaur had actual fossilized skin which indicates that this animal may have had stripes along its tail.

WOW

Camouflage is important in every animal and insect in our world. It is difficult for Scientists to know exactly how dinosaurs camouflaged within their environment as very little is around today. However, by looking at todays animals and insects we can speculate on how dinosaurs may have acted. Can you see the butterfly feeding on nectar in this picture?

GIANT PLANT-EATERS

Within this section we explore some of the most awesomely massive dinosaurs ever to exist – the giant plant-eating sauropods.

INTRODUCING ...

BRACHIOSAURUS

ARGENTINOSAURUS

DIPLODOCUS

APATOSAURUS

SEISMOSAURUS

HADROSAURUS

MELANOROSAURUS

SALTASAURUS

TITANOSAURUS

CAMARASAURUS

ULTRASAURUS

BRACHIOSAURUS

Brachiosaurus was once thought to be the biggest ever dinosaur until the discovery of other dinosaurs such as Argentinosaurus. Brachiosaurus was discovered in 1900 and fossils have been found in the USA and Africa. They probably moved around in large family herds (like elephants) and lived during the late Jurassic Period. They were herbivores (vegetarians) and would have eaten ferns and bushes and grazed the tree-tops with its long neck.

WOWZER IT'S HUGE!

Look how this Brachiosaurus compares with a man standing underneath it. They were massive, weighing a whopping 70 tonnes (20 times that of a large elephant measuring 82 ft (25 m) long and standing tall at 49 ft (15 m) high.

GREEDY DINO

The Brachiosaurus had to eat about 200 kg (440 lb) of food (greens) EVERY DAY just to fuel its massive body. If eating your greens can let you grow this big then there are no excuses when it comes to eating your broccoli at dinner!
So they could digest all this food these dinosaurs also swallowed STONES (hmm tasty) which helped grind down the tough leaves and plant fibres.

DID YOU KNOW?

Each Brachiosaurus may well have lived to be over 100 years old.

COME AND SEE ME

If you visit Chicago O'Hare international airport in the U.S.A. you can see a full size Brachiosaurus. It is 75 feet long and 40 feet high. This is an exact replica made out of fibreglass of a fossil that was unearthed in the Grand Junction, Colarado in 1900.

HERD INSTINCT

Brachiosaurus probably travelled in herds with others. This wasn't because they were sociable creatures, but because by travelling with lots of others they were less likely to be the one that got attacked and more likely to have others help if it was.

GENTLE GIANT WITH A BIG HEART

So that blood could be pumped all the way up the long neck of the Brachiosaurus they needed a very large and muscular heart. Because of the difficulty of pumping blood around such a large animal some scientists believe that the Brachiosaurus must have been warm-blooded, whilst others believe the neck was always kept parallel to the floor (i.e. never raised above the body) and some even thought that it lived in water, although this was later disproven.

ARGENTINOSAURUS

If you thought the Brachiosaurus was large then the Argentinosaurus is massive! It is believed to be the biggest ever land-dwelling animal ever, a true GIANT. The largest living animal today is the Blue Whale.

WOW – AMAZING

Because of its long neck the Argentinosaurus would have easily been able to peer in through a fourth storey window of a skyscraper!

ARGENTINOSAURUS vs THE BLUE WHALE

LIVES: Argentina, South America vs Artic Oceans

TIME: Lived in Late Cretaceaous period, now extinct vs Still alive today although critically endangered

LENGTH: 130 ft head to tail (40 m) 100 ft (9m tall, vs 30.5 m) from head to tail

WEIGHT: 90-110 Tons vs 150-200 Tons

ARGENTINA – THE LAND OF THE GIANTS

Some of the worlds largest dinosaurs have been found in South America, in particular Argentina. The largest meat-eating dinosaur, the scary Giganotosaurus, lived at the same time as the largest ever dinosaur Argentinosaurus. As the Giganotosaurus may have hunted in packs it may have hunted down the Argentinosaurus, a truly gigantic fight.

DID YOU KNOW?

It's length was as long as four buses.

BIG BOY... BIG POOP

Just like the Braciosaurus the Argentinosaurus had to eat a massive amount to fuel its gigantic body. It would have spent most of its life constantly eating.
In Patagonia, Argentina at this time finding food would not have been hard, it was a lush land full of conifers, seeds, fruits and flowering plants.
Scientists have estimated that the Argentinosaurus would have pooped at least 15 liters volume of dung!!!

DIPLODOCUS

The name Diplodocus means 'double beamed lizard' and comes from the fact that the bones in the middle of its tail run both backward and forward. Diplodocus is a quadruped and each foot had five toes, and one toe on each foot had a claw, which could've been used as self-defense.

Although it was massive and scary in size it didn't like meat and, as a herbivore, used to spend virtually all day long eating leaves and foliage such as ferns. However, Diplodocus couldn't chew, so he swallowed small stones to help grind up the food inside its stomach.

DID YOU KNOW?

The only fossils of Diplodocus to have been found so far are in North America in Colorado, Montana, Utah and Wyoming. This is not to say that they didn't live anywhere else, but based on what has been found, Diplodocus was a true American!

86

SAY IT PROPERLY

It's not prononuced
di-PLOD-oh-kuss
but
dip-LOW-doe-kuss.

FACTS CHANGE WITH TIME

Early research suggested that Diplodocus might have swum in water but more recent studies have indicated that the massive water pressure on the chest would have made it too difficult for the Diplodocus to breathe out of its nostrils.

It used to be thought that the sauropods (like Diplodocus) had a second brain. Palaeontologists now think that what they thought was a second brain was simply a large spinal cord in the hip area.

DIPLODOCUS STATS

NAME: Diplodocus
HEIGHT: 20 ft (6 m)
LENGTH: 89 ft (27 m)
SPECIAL FEATURES: Long neck, whiplash tail, hollow bones, tiny head.

AWESOME!

Diplodocus was one of the longest animals ever to have lived on planet earth!

AWESOME FACT!

Some palaeontologists believe that Diplodocus used his tails as a weapon. However, due to its massive size, physicists have shown that were that the case, the speed achieved at the very tip of the tail would have broken the sound barrier!

APATOSAURUS

Apatosaurus is another famous North American giant Herbivore that grazed the plains during the Jurassic Period, 150 million years ago. Just like the Diplodocus the Apatosaurus had peg-like teeth ideal for stripping leaves. As it would have eaten almost constantly when awake to fuel its massive body, it was lucky to have nostrils on top of its skull so that it could eat and breathe at the same time.

MMMM TASTY

Big dinosaurs like the Apatosaurus would have swallowed stones to help with digestion by grinding up tough leaves and fibrous plants, these stones were called Gastroliths.

THE DINOSAUR FORMERLY KNOWN AS BRONTOSAURUS

Apatosaurus means 'deceptive lizard' and was found and named by the famous paleontologist Othniel Marsh in 1877. In 1879 he found and named a new dinosaur called Brontosaurus, however in 1903 it was discovered that Brontosaurus was just a fully-grown Apatosaurus. Despite this the name Brontosaurus is still popular and was not removed from the official naming list until 1974.

QUICK FACTS:

Length:	69 - 90 ft (21 - 27 m)
Height at hip:	10-15 ft (3 - 5 m)
Weight:	27 tons

THE MAN-EATING HERBIVORE

In the 1933 movie King Kong, the Apatosaurus was portrayed as a blood-thirsty Carnivore not as the gentle plant-eating dinosaur we know it to be. Don't believe everything you see in the movies!

A BIG WALKING JUICY PIECE OF STEAK

Or so the Allosaurus that hunted the Apatosaurus thought. Allosaurus tooth marks have been found in the fossilised vertebrae of the Apatosaurus. However, the Apatosaurus had a trick up its sleeve for protection, it was so large that when it lifted its head the Allosaurus would not have been able to reach its head or neck, the most vulnerable parts of its body.

BIG FOOT

Forget Big Foot the mysterious ape like creature, some Apatosaurus footprints found have been around 1 m across!

EGGS AWAY!

Some scientists believe that as these giant dinosaurs were so large and their eggs also large they simply laid the eggs as they walked along and did not need to look after them.

SEISMOSAURUS

Known as 'earthquake lizard', Seismosaurus was named because its massive size would have shaken the earth with every step it took.

It was discovered in 1979 but because of its gigantic size and the large rocks where the fossil was found, it took 13 years for archaeologists to excavate it. Finally in 1991 David Gillette, who originally discovered it 14 years earlier, was able to formally name it as Seismosaurus.

WOW - REALLY?

Seismosaurus probably hatched from eggs like other sauropods. They are also thought to have lived to be 100 years old, giving them a very long lifespan compared to other dinosaurs.

STOMACH OF STONE

In 1979 the fossilized bones of a Seismosaurus were discovered in New Mexico, USA. Palentologists found more than 200 'Gastroliths'. Gastroliths are small stones and palaeontologists believe that Seismosaurus swallowed these stones to help digest its food, just like the cold-blooded reptile living today, the Crocodile, which also swallows small stones to digest its food.

WHAT A TRAGIC END!

The specimen found at this site is believed to have tragically died by swallowing a stone that was too large and which lodged in its throat and blocked its ability to breathe.

DID YOU KNOW?

Seismosaurus' long neck would have usually been held parallel to the ground. It might have allowed the creature to poke its head into dense forest areas to reach leaves otherwise inaccessible to bulky dinosaurs, or maybe to eat soft pteridophytes that grew in wet areas too swampy to enter safely.

HOW LONG?

Seismosaurus is at the top of the 'longest dinosaur' list at around 110 ft or 33.5 m.

HADROSAURUS

Although this dinosaur could arguably be said to resemble a much larger version of our modern day horse, the name Hadrosaurus means 'Heavy Lizard'.

In 1838 Hadrosaurus was unintentionally discovered, in Haddonfield, New Jersey, USA hidden in a marl (claypit). It was initially uncovered by a Mr John Hopkins, who found massive, giant bones, but thought nothing of them and took them back to his family house, where he put them in a cabinet.

Some 20 years later a visitor, called William Foulke, spotted the bones in 1858 and he then went to the pit and started to explore further. Foulke then made contact with Joseph Leidy, a paleontologist. They recovered the fossils and it was named Hadrosaurus Foulkii, in honour of Foulke.

DID YOU KNOW?

Hadrosaurus was the first almost complete dinosaur to be discovered on the earth. It was also the first ever dinosaur fossil to be mounted and put on display in a museum.

HE WAS RIGHT!

Long before this in 1841, a British man, Dr Richard Owen started to suggest that these large bones likely belonged to a group of large reptiles that had become extinct from the earth, he called them Dinosaurs, meaning terrible lizards. However, no-one believed him.

HOW DO YOU SAY MY NAME

Had-row-sawr-us

AWESOME HISTORY

In October 2003, a bronze statue of Hadrosaurus was completed in the state of New Jersey. This statue was created to the same size as Hadrosaurus would have been. It was unveiled in Haddonfield, near to where the first Hadrosaurus was found.

MELANOROSAURUS

Melanorosaurus means 'Black Mountain Lizard' and it lived in the early Triassic Period around 225-205 million years ago in the woodlands of South Africa. Melanorosaurus was a plant-eater and had a bulky body, long neck and tail, a relatively small skull and brain and erect limbs which would looked a bit like the limbs of an elephant. Its diet would have consisted of branches, leaves and twigs which, given its height and long neck, would have been easy to reach from the tops of trees. Serrated leaf-shaped teeth would have allowed it to snap off branches and then chew the vegetation quite effectively before swallowing.

LARGEST OF ITS TIME!

Melanorosaurus was the biggest dinosaur of the Triassic Era! At 39 ft or 12 m long and weighing around 5,000 lbs or 2250 kg it was the largest dinosaur of its day. It was only in the Cretaceous Period and later that larger dinosaurs have been found.

DID YOU KNOW?

It would have had the ability to walk on two legs but it didn't have to, this is called a facultative biped. It may have taken advantage of this skill to reach high up tasty leaves!

BONE FACT

Whilst its limbs had dense bones, its spinal bones and vertebrae were hollow to reduce their weight.

FOSSIL FACT

Melanorosaurus pronounced meh-lan-oh-roe-sore-us, was named by the British paleontologist Sydney H. Haugh in 1924. It was named after the Thaba Nyama or 'Black Mountain' in South Africa where the fossil was found.

iPad

SALTASAURUS

Saltasaurus, a herbivore, belonged to the Sauropod group, which meant that it had a long neck, small head and lengthy tail. However fossil discoveries have shown that Saltasaurus was smaller than most other dinoaurs within the Sauropod group.

Saltasaurus had a smaller neck and legs than most other herbivore dinosaurs and this would have presented immediate problems, such as being unable to reach high tree branches and this meant less food.

COOL!

The name Saltasaurus, means 'Lizard from Salta'. The first Saltasaurus was discovered in Salta, Argentina in 1980 by José Bonaparte and Jaime Powell.

DEFENSIVE ARMOR PLATING

Saltasaurus is currently the only discovered Sauropod who had armor plating. Both its back and side were covered in circular and oval bony plates up to 5 in (12 cm) in diameter. It is also possible that horns or spikes may have stuck out for extra defense. It is likely that the armor and then any spikes were slowly introduced to the Saltasaurus as a result of evolution due to its inferior size compared to other large plant-eaters. Saltasaurus has now been reclassified as an ankylosaur.

DID YOU KNOW?

Communal nest-building shows that Saltasaurus probably lived and travelled in herds.

HOW DO YOU SAY MY NAME?

salt-ah-sawr-us

TITANOSAURUS

Titanosaurus means 'titanic lizard' and was a sauropod dinosaur, much like Argentinosaurus. It lived in the woodlands of Asia, Europe, Africa and South America during the late Cretaceous Period around 80-65 million years ago. Titanosaurus had a bulky body, a long 'whiplash' tail and a tiny head on a very long neck. It would have weighed in around 15 tons and had a very wide chest which placed its legs very widely apart. Although it would have walked on four legs, it had a very flexible spine which would have allowed it rear up on its hind legs to reach high up in the branches to eat leaves.

EGGS!

Although Titanosaurus eggs were only about 5 in or 12 cm across, the babies that hatched would grow to be longer than a bus. It is thought that eggs where laid in large nesting grounds and buried under vegetation.

POOP!

The fossilised remains of Titanosaurus dung show that it ate pretty much any plant material. Remains from conifer twigs and leaves, palms and grasses where found in its poop!

DID YOU KNOW?

Fossilized impressions of Titanosaurus skin have survived and we know that it had armor to protect it. Its skin was covered with a pattern of small bead-like scales surrounding larger scales.

FOSSIL FINDS

Richard Lydekker named Titanosaurus in 1877 almost 20 years after the first remains were first discovered. In May 2006, Italian scientists found four well-preserved Titanosaurus skeletons in South America.

HOW DO YOU SAY MY NAME?

Tie-tan-oh-sawr-us

CAMARASAURUS

Camarasaurus means 'chambered lizard' and it lived during the late Jurassic Period around 155 to 145 million years ago. Camarasaurus looked a bit like Diplodocus with a long neck and tail. It was a large herbivore and although it wasn't as big as other sauropods it still weighed up to 20 tons!

CAMARASAURUS DATA

PRONUNICATION:
kuh-mare-UH-SAWR-US
DIET: Plant-eater
FEATURES: Spoon shaped teeth

DID YOU KNOW?

The name 'chambered lizard' comes from the holes in the vertebrae that decrease its weight.

CAMARASAURUS FOSSILS

Camarasaurus fossils have been found in Colorado, New Mexico, Utah, and Wyoming. Camarasaurus was named in 1877 by Edward Drinker Cope.

SCAN ME
Instructions on page 5

ULTRASAURUS

Ultrasaurus, meaning 'ultra lizard' was believed to be over 60 ft (18.2m) tall and 100 ft (30.5m) long making it one of the largest dinosaurs found. However, only limited bones were found and it might actually be composed of two separate dinosaurs, the shoulder blade from Brachiosaurus and a shoulder bone from Supersaurus.

DID YOU KNOW?

Ultrasaurus would have needed a very powerful heart to pump blood around its massive body.

CONFUSED?

The name was originally given to a sauropod that was found in Colorado, USA and was then given to another fossil in Asia. However it turned out the fossil in Asia was a lot smaller than the first fossil. The discovery in Colorado was one of the largest dinosaurs ever found and is now officially known as Supersaurus.

COLD-BLOODED CREATURES

People disagree over whether dinosaurs were cold-blooded or warm-blooded. It used to be believed that dinosaurs were cold-blooded like their reptile ancestors. Paleontologists have recently argued that at least some of the dinosaurs were fast, active, competed against warm-blooded mammals, lived in cool areas, were related to birds and therefore conclude they were warm-blooded.

WHAT ARE WARM-BLOODED CREATURES?

Warm-blooded creatures include humans, mammals and birds. They regulate the temperature inside their bodies to a constant temperature. Warm-bloods generate heat when they are in a cooler environment, and cool themselves when they are in a hotter environment. To generate heat, warm-blooded animals convert the food they eat into energy. Warm-bloods eat a lot of food compared with their cold-blooded relations and most of this food is used to fuel a constant body temperature.

FACT FOR THE WARM-BLOOD CASE

Many of the big dinosaurs like T-Rex and Iguanodon held their heads high above their bodies. To do this they would have needed two blood circuits and an internally divided heart which would make them warm-blooded.

WHAT ARE COLD-BLOODED ANIMALS?

Cold-blooded creatures include reptiles, insects, arachnids, amphibians and fish. They take on the temperature of their surroundings, for example when the environment is hot they are hot and when the environment is cold they are cold. Cold-blooded animals are much slower in cold environments, their muscle activity is dependent on chemical reactions which function much more quickly in hotter temperatures. They are often found sunning themselves in the morning to warm up and get going.

FACT FOR THE COLD-BLOOD CASE

Dinosaurs like Spinosaurus and Ouranosaurus had large sails on their backs, they probably used these for collection and removal of heat which suggests they were cold-blooded.

DID YOU KNOW?

In 2000 the fossil of a Thescelosaurus was found to have a mammal-like four chambered heart suggesting it was warm-blooded.

DINOSAURS IN THE SEA

This group are not technically dinosaurs but marine reptiles. However, like dinosaurs, some reached vast sizes some up to 58 ft or 17.6 m long!

INTRODUCING ...

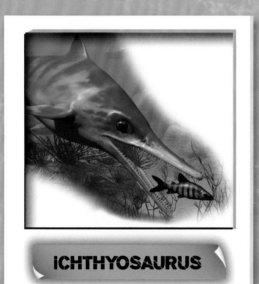

ICHTHYOSAURUS

ELASMOSAURUS

KRONOSAURUS

TYLOSAURUS

MOSASAURUS

OPTHALMOSAURUS

PLESIOSAURUS

NOTHOSAURUS

LIOPLEURADON

SHONISAURUS

ICHTHYOSAURUS

Ichthyosaurus was an ichthyosaur, a marine reptile, and was not a dinosaur as such. Ichthyosaurus lived from the early Jurassic Period until the early Cretaceous Period, roughly 206 to 140 million years ago. Ichthyosaurus' diet was mostly fish, but may have also included cephalopods. It had an amazingly fishlike shape, with a streamlined body, a finlike structure on its back, and a two-pronged tail, it looked a bit like a bluefin tuna.

WOW SPEEDY

Ichthyosaurus was about 6.5 ft or 2 m long and and would have weighed about 200 lbs or 90 kg. This sleek animal may have swum at speeds up to 25 mph (40 kph).

SPEEDO®

DID YOU KNOW?

Hundreds of Ichthyosaurus fossils have been found in England, Germany, Greenland, and Alberta, Canada. Ichthyosaurus, which means 'fish lizard,' was named by Charles Koenig in 1818.

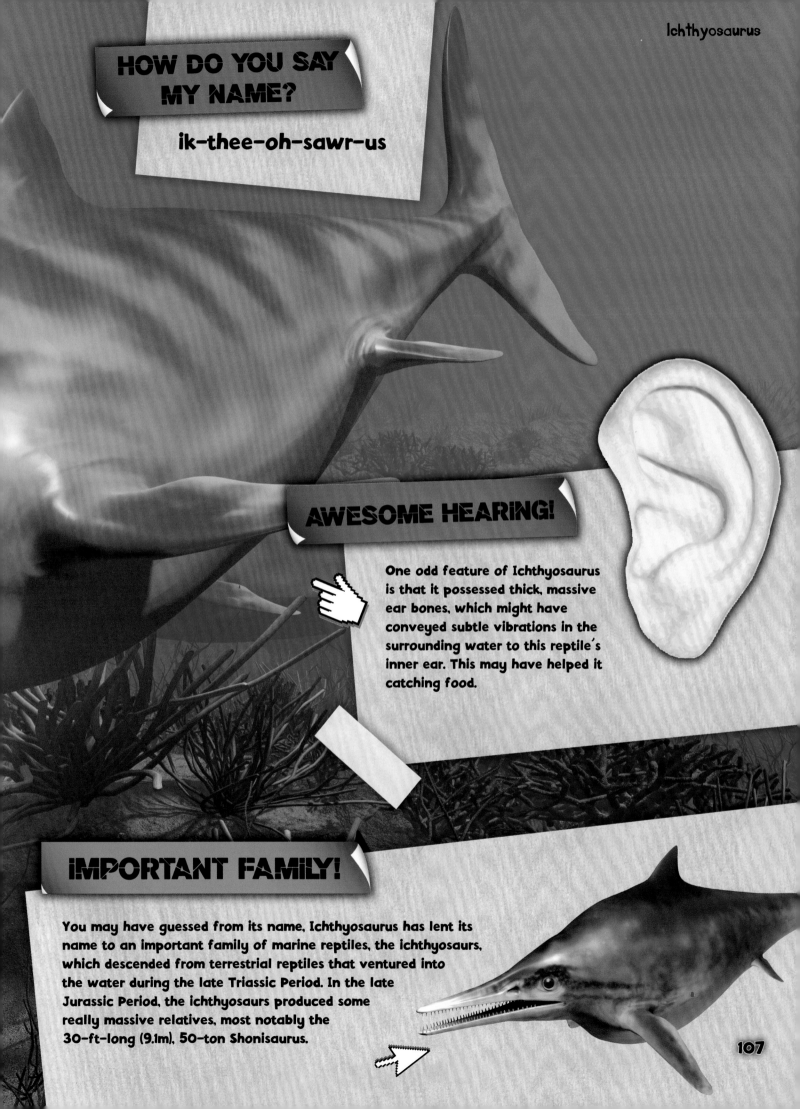

HOW DO YOU SAY MY NAME?

ik-thee-oh-sawr-us

AWESOME HEARING!

One odd feature of Ichthyosaurus is that it possessed thick, massive ear bones, which might have conveyed subtle vibrations in the surrounding water to this reptile's inner ear. This may have helped it catching food.

IMPORTANT FAMILY!

You may have guessed from its name, Ichthyosaurus has lent its name to an important family of marine reptiles, the ichthyosaurs, which descended from terrestrial reptiles that ventured into the water during the late Triassic Period. In the late Jurassic Period, the ichthyosaurs produced some really massive relatives, most notably the 30-ft-long (9.1m), 50-ton Shonisaurus.

ELASMOSAURUS

Elasmosaurus meaning 'ribbon lizard' was a long-necked marine reptile that was up to 46 ft or 14 m long. It lived in the Late Cretaceous around 70 million years ago. Half of its length was its neck, which had as many as 75-76 vertebrae in it! Elasmosaurus had four long, paddle-like flippers, a tiny head, sharp teeth in strong jaws, and a pointed tail. It was the longest of the Plesiosaurs.

YOU'LL NEVER GUESS WHAT!

The land mass in the late Cretaceous Period was very different from today, the first fossil of the plesiosaur Elasmosaurus was discovered in 1868 in landlocked Kansas – not the first place you'd think to dig up a marine reptile! 70 million years ago, much of North America was submerged beneath the Western Interior Sea, and many remains of icthyosaurs, plesiosaurs and mosasaurs have been found.

HOW DID IT EAT?

Elasmosaurus had an enormously long neck which could be 25 ft long, that's 4 times longer than a giraffe's neck! This unusual feature has led to some disagreement about how Elasmosaurus hunted for fish. Some paleontologists think it bent its head sideways around its body, while others believe this reptile swam on the surface, holding its head high above the water to scope out prey.

WHICH END IS THE HEAD!

Elasmosaurus was the cause of one of the pettier disputes in 19th-century paleontology, the Bone Wars, which started with a Cretaceous bang when the famous fossil-hunter Edward Drinker Cope mistook this plesiosaur's long neck for its tail — and placed the head on the wrong end! Cope's rival Othniel C. Marsh took great pleasure in pointing out the error, and the two paleontologists spent the rest of the 19th century in a bitter feud.

HOW DO YOU SAY MY NAME?

ee-laz-moh-sawr-us

KRONOSAURUS

Kronosaurus lived during the Middle Cretaceous Period around 110 million years ago. Kronosaurus was a classic example of a pliosaur, marine reptiles characterized by their enormous thick heads, short necks, stocky trunks and outsized flippers. Kronosaurus lived in the seas that covered parts of Australia.

WOW GREEDY

Kronosaurus appears to be much like a modern Great White Shark, simply eating anything, fish, squid, and other marine reptiles, that swam across its path. It was fast and fierce and one of the top predators of the ancient ocean. The 'Kronos' in this giant's name derives from the ancient Greek god, who ate his own children in an attempt to preserve his power.

BIG BUT NOT THAT BIG!

Although Kronosaurus was big it didn't approach the bulk of the most massive pliosaur of all time, Liopleurodon, which may have weighed as much as 35 tons compared to about 10 tons for the largest Kronosaurus individuals. Both of these reptiles were outclassed by the giant shark Megalodon, which lived tens of millions of years later and attained weights in the 50 ton range.

WOW FACT

Kronosaurus lived in the open oceans and breathed air. Some Plesiosaurs have been found with small stones in their stomachs, these may have been used to help grind up their food, or as extra weight, to help them dive. They probably laid eggs in beach sand like modern-day sea turtles.

SCAN ME
Instructions on page 5

DID YOU KNOW?

Kronosaurus means 'Kronos lizard', pronounced crow-no-SORE-us. Kronosaurus fossils have been found in Australia and Colombia, South America. It was discovered in Queensland, Australia, in 1889 by A. Crombie and was originally thought to be an ichthyosaur. It was named and described by Longman in 1924.

TYLOSAURUS

Tylosaurus was a large, predatory marine lizard closely related to modern monitor lizards and snakes living in the Late Cretaceous Period around 85–80 million years ago. Fossils have been found in North America and New Zealand. These giant sea hunters ate other sea creatures, such as fish, shellfish, smaller mosasaurs, turtles and even diving pteranodons that got too close to the sea surface.

AWESOME

Tylosaurus rarely bit off more that it could chew – it was able to flex its lower jaw allowing it to open its mouth very wide and swallow large prey in one piece, just like a modern- day snake!

HOW BIG?

Tylosaurus was a marine reptile known as a mosasaur. It was one of the biggest of the mosasaurs, growing up to 39 ft or 13 m long - that's as long as a double-decker bus!

DID YOU KNOW?

The name Tylosaurus comes from the Greek words 'tylos' – knob or protuberance and 'sauros' – lizard. It is named after its remarkable long and almost cylindrical nose that has a round and bony end. It also had bony plates on its head and scales all over its body.

AND THE WINNER WAS!

Like Elasmosaurus, Tylosaurus figured in the famous 19th-century Bone Wars between the famous paleontologists Othniel C. Marsh and Edward Drinker Cope. Arguing over a set of incomplete Tylosaurus fossils, Marsh suggested the name Rhinosaurus 'nose lizard', a missed opportunity if ever there was one! Cope suggested Rhamposaurus instead, but this name was already taken. It was left to Charles Sternberg in 1918, to make an amazing Tylosaurus discovery, with the remains of a plesiosaur in its stomach.

MOSASAURUS

The fearsome Mosasaurus was a giant member of the family of marine reptiles known as mosasaurs, which had big alligator-like heads, powerful jaws, streamlined bodies and front and rear flippers. It lived during the Late Cretaceous Period around 70-65 million years ago. It frequented shallow seas and is directly related to monitor lizards.

ONE OF THE EARLIEST!

Mosasaurus is named after the River Meuse near Maastricht in the Netherlands, where the first fossil specimen was found. It was given the name in 1822 and Mosasaurus were some of the earliest dinosaur fossils to be discovered. These discoveries led early naturalists to identify for the first time that currently extinct species had once lived on the earth, which went against the accepted religious beliefs at the time.

FANCY A DRINK!

In 1795, a Mosasaurus skull was traded to the occupying French army for 600 bottles of wine! It sits in a Paris museum.

WHAT'S FOR LUNCH?

The preserved stomach contents of Mosasaurus fossils show them to have eaten sharks, bony fish, turtles and other marine reptiles. It was one of the most ferocious aquatic predators of its time.

SWAM LIKE AN EEL

Mosasaurus had about 100 vertebrae in its back each joined to the next by a flexible ball-and-socket joint. This would have allowed Mosasaurus to move in the water like an eel.

DID THEY, DIDN'T THEY!

Scientists cannot agree as to whether Mosasaurus came onto land to lay eggs, like turtles, or gave birth to live young in the water.

OPTHALMOSAURUS

The name Ophthalmosaurus means 'eye lizard'. It lived during the Late Jurassic Period 165–150 million years ago. Although it was perfectly adapted for living in the water, Ophthalmosaurus needed to breathe air, like a dolphin or whale does today. It was not a true dinosaur, but a marine reptile.

WOW FACT

Although Ophthalmosaurus could dive to great depths (maybe even as deep as 3 miles!), it may have paid the a price for doing so. Fossil evidence shows clear signs of what modern deep-sea divers call the bends – when a diver ascends too quickly, decompressed nitrogen in the blood forms painful bubbles that can damage tissue and even bone.

HOW DO YOU SAY MY NAME?

Off-thal-moh-saw-rus.

DID YOU KNOW?

Ophthalmosaurus could not get onto land to lay eggs, instead they gave birth to live young in the water. Their young, which are called 'pups' were born tail-first to prevent them drowning. We know this because fossils survive of females in the act of giving birth.

AS YOU MAY HAVE GUESSED

What set Ophthalmosaurus apart from other ichthyosaurs were its eyes, which were huge – up to 9 in or 23 cm – compared to the rest of its body. As in other marine reptiles, these eyes were encircled by bony structures called sclerotic rings, which allowed the eyeballs to maintain their spherical shape in conditions of extreme water pressure.

WHY SUCH BIG EYES?

Most likely so it could locate prey in very deep water, where a marine creature's eyes have to be very efficient in order to feed in the very scarce light. It may have also been a night hunter.
Fossils have been found in Europe and Argentina. The earliest find was made by a British scientist Harry Seeley in 1874.

PLESIOSAURUS

Plesiosaurus meaning 'near lizard' and pronounced plee-zee-oh-SAWR-us, was one of a number of marine reptiles that lived at the same time at the dinosaurs in the Early-Middle Jurassic Period around 135-120 million years ago. These streamlined reptiles were about 7.6 ft or 2.3 m long and may have weighed about 200 lbs or 90 kg. They had four wide, paddle-shaped flippers, and a tapered body. They had many long, sharp, conical teeth in long jaws. The head was relatively small.

DID YOU KNOW?

Plesiosaurus fossils were amongst some of the earliest fossil discoveries and Plesiosaurus created a sensation back in the early 19th century, as scientists didn't know quite what to make of it! It was first found by the famous fossil hunter Mary Anning in 1821 and was later named by H.T. De La Beche and William D. Conybeare. Plesiosaurus fossils have been found in England and Germany. In 2004 a fully intact fossilised young Plesiosaurus was found about 31 miles north of where the first Plesiosaurus was found.

NOT THE BEST!

Plesiosaurus probably wasn't the most accomplished of swimmers, they lacked the hydrodynamic shapes of their bigger, meaner and more streamlined cousins, the pliosaurs.

ONE OF THE FIRST!

The first Plesiosaurus fossil was found long before the first dinosaur fossil.

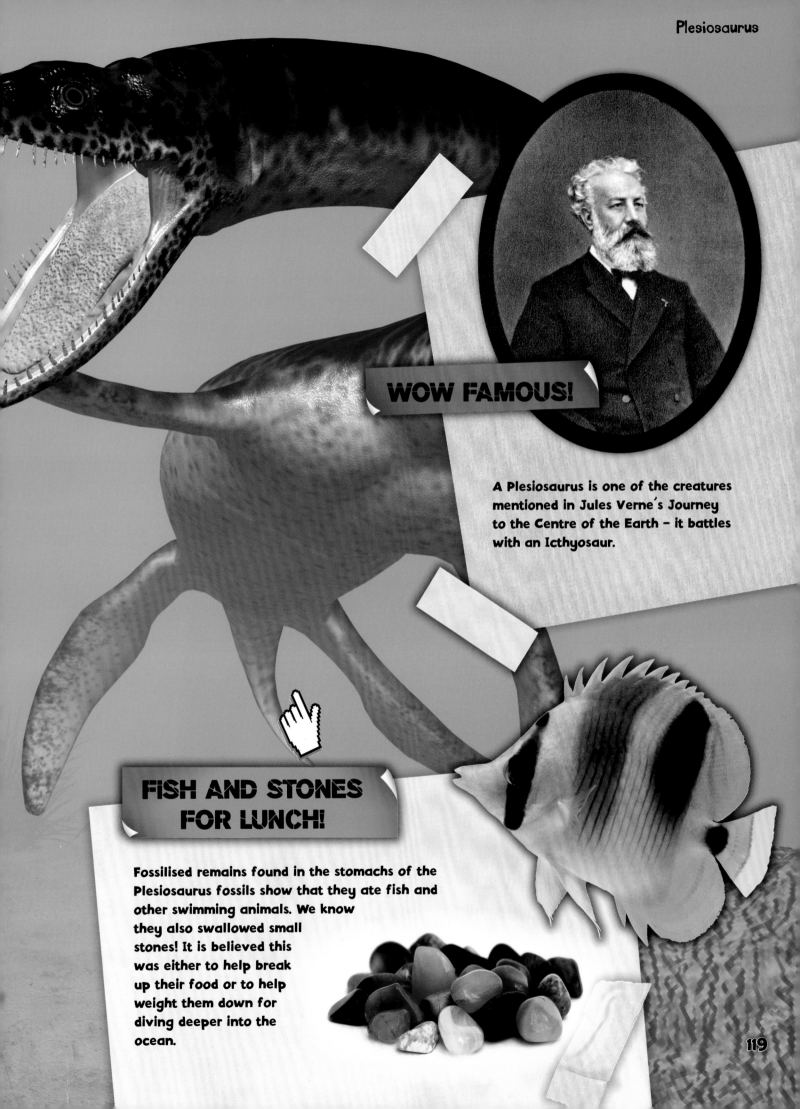

WOW FAMOUS!

A Plesiosaurus is one of the creatures mentioned in Jules Verne's Journey to the Centre of the Earth – it battles with an Icthyosaur.

FISH AND STONES FOR LUNCH!

Fossilised remains found in the stomachs of the Plesiosaurus fossils show that they ate fish and other swimming animals. We know they also swallowed small stones! It is believed this was either to help break up their food or to help weight them down for diving deeper into the ocean.

NOTHOSAURUS

Nothosaurs were long-necked, long-tailed, fish-eating reptiles ranging from a few inches to 20 ft or 6 m long. Nothosaurs lived during the Triassic period, around 250-210 million years ago and went extinct during the late Triassic Period. They may have evolved into the plesiosaurs. Nothosaurs had four wide, paddle-like limbs with webbed fingers and toes. These reptiles had a long, thin head with many sharp teeth; the front teeth were longer than the back teeth. The nostrils were on the top end of the snout. They breathed air but spent most of the time in the water.

Nothosaurus, did not live in water all the time like its descendants the later plesiosaurs. It would have come up onto rocks and beaches, just like a seal to rest. It's clear that this creature breathed air, as evidenced by the two nostrils on the top end of its nose, and although it was undoubtedly a good swimmer, it wasn't as well adapted to a full-time aquatic lifestyle as later pliosaurs and plesiosaurs like Elasmosaurus to which it was distantly related.

DIET

Fish and shrimp

WOW SHARP

Small, sharp teeth lined its jaws all the way to the back of its cheeks. These interlocking teeth acted like a trap for fish and once it got a grip Nothosaurus did not easily let go! Nothosaurus means 'false lizard' and is pronounced no-tho-SORE-us. It was not a dinosaur at all, in spite of its lizard-like apprearance. It is one of a whole group of reptiles called nothosaurs. This group was named by G von Meunster in 1834.

GOOD SWIMMER!

Powerful legs and a strong tail made Nothosaurus a very strong swimmer.

121

LIOPLEURADON

Liopleuradon lived in the mid to late Jurassic period throughout Europe. Liopleuradon had huge flippers that propelled it through the water. It was a type of short-necked plesiosaur – a type of reptile that had returned to the sea. A successful hunter, it had a set of long jaws and needle-sharp teeth. It would of probably of eaten marine crocodiles, the giant fish Leedsichthys, Ichthyosaurs and possibly other pliosaurs.

Liopleuradon was probably the biggest predator that's ever lived in the sea. It was 82 ft or 25 m long that's big as a swimming pool!

DID YOU KNOW?

As it was a successful hunter, it would of had a set of long jaws and needle-sharp teeth. It probably would of preyed on marine crocodiles, giant fish, and other pliosaurs.

WHAT'S THAT SMELL!

Liopleuradon had nostrils in its skull, which allowed it to smell its prey in the water.

SHONISAURUS

Shonisaurus means 'Shoshone mountain reptile' and is pronounced show-nih-SORE-us. It lived during Late Triassic period around 225-208 million years ago. Like other ichthyosaurs, Shonisaurus is believed to have evolved from land-dwelling lizards that returned to an aquatic lifestyle during the early Triassic period. Shonisaurus fossils have been found in land-locked Nevada, which was submerged beneath a shallow body of water during much of the Mesozoic Era.

AS BIG AS A WHALE!

Shonisaurus was an ichtyosaur and looked very much like a dolphin. However, its body was a huge 49 ft or 15 m long so it was more like a whale in size.

NICE PLATES!

Miners discovered the first bones of the Shonisaurus and it is thought they used its backbone segments as dinner plates!

ATTACK AND DEFENSE

Dinosaurs attacked each other, defended themselves and competed for leadership within groups. Even though some of the dinosaurs could be deadly most of them where peaceful herbivores that never attacked.

By the end of the Cretaceous Period, after millions of years of being attacked by tyrannosaurs, raptors, and other fierce hunters evolution produced some of the most heavily armed defensive animals the world has ever seen: Ankylosaurs.

SCAN ME
Instructions on page 5

IN THE CORNER FOR ATTACK!

Teeth. Most predators would use their teeth as a weapon to maim or kill their prey. Giganotosaurus (see page 32) had teeth which measured up to 8 in or 20 cm and these were well adapted for slicing into flesh. T-rex (see page 30) had 58 serrated teeth which re-grew when damaged making it a fearsome attacker. Palaeontologists believe that some of tyrannosaurs teeth were shaped to gather shreds of the meat it ate. As the shreds rotted, they bred dangerous bacteria, meaning any non-fatal bite would result in an infected, gangrenous wound. All T-rex then had to do was wait for its prey to die from infected wound and pick up its supper!

Claws. It's unlikely that a dinosaur would have killed its prey with claws alone. However the claws would have been used to grab its prey and keep it in a death grip. Baryonyx had large, powerful claws on their front hands, which they most probably used to slash prey. Deinonychus (see page 36) had single, oversized, curved claws on their feet.

Eyesight and smell. Troodon (see page 56) had large eyes and relatively advanced binocular vision, making it easier for them to zero in on prey. Some dinosaurs such as T-rex had an advanced sense of smell, which allowed them to scent prey from a long distance away.

Force. Tyrannosaurs were built a bit like a battering ram, with massive heads, thick bodies, and powerful legs. An attacking T-rex could knock its victim clean off its feet, provided it had the element of surprise. Once a victim like Stegosaurus was on its back, stunned, the tyrannosaur could move in for the kill.

IN THE CORNER FOR DEFENSE!

Tails. The long, flexible tails of sauropods could be used like whips, delivering stunning blows to approaching predators. Ankylosaurus (see page 110) had the best defensive tail with its mace like growths at the ends of their tails that could crush the skulls and bones of its enemies.

Armor. No creatures on earth were more geared up to defend themselves from attack than Ankylosaurus who even had armored eyelids! By the time the dinosaurs became extinct, even some of the sauropods had developed light armor, which may have helped fend off attacks by packs of smaller raptors.

Size. Sauropods grew to such massive sizes that they were virtually immune to predators, even a pack of adult Velociraptors would have a bit of trouble taking down a 110-ton Argentinosaurus.

Speed. Whilst the massive sauropods weren't able to run very fast, most of the hadrosaurs could rise onto their back legs and run away. Some smaller plant eating dinosaurs may have been capable of sprinting at least 30 or 40 miles per hour, especially when being chased.

Hearing. Generally, predators have superior sight and smell, while prey animals have acute hearing, so they can run away if they hear an unfamiliar sound. It is known that Hadrosaurs (see page 80) could make sounds and it's likely they bellowed to each other, warning the entire herd about an approaching tyrannosaur.

ARMORED DINOSAURS

Within the next pages you will see some of the best defensive dinosaurs ever to have lived. These guys are the armored SUVs of the dinosaur world!

INTRODUCING ...

STEGOSAURUS

ANKYLOSAURUS

KENTROSAURUS

EDMONTONIA

SCELIDOSAURUS

SCUTELLOSAURUS

NODOSAURUS

MINMI

PANOPLOSAURUS

SHONISAURUS

STEGOSAURUS

The Stegosaurus is the most famous dinosaur from a group of dinosaurs known as Stegosauria. The Stegosaurus was a large dinosaur that featured unique bones and plates along its spine. They were all herbivores (plant eaters) and featured rows of unique bones that developed into plates and spines along their back and tail.

GUESS WHAT?

The Stegosaurus also featured tail spikes that reached around 2ft (60cm) to 3ft (90cm) in length. Along with Tyrannosaurus Rex and Iguanodon, Stegosaurus was one of three dinosaurs that inspired the appearance of Godzilla.

MPH

60 80

40 100

20

120

0

140

000108

SUPER FACT!

Researchers believe that due to the nature of Stegosaurus' legs, they had a maximum speed of around 5 mph (7 kph). The 17 plates found along the back of the Stegosaurus arose from the skin rather than being attached to the skeleton. The largest plates were around 2 ft (60 cm) tall and 2 ft (60 cm) wide.

SCAN ME
Instructions on page 5

MEGA COOL!

Stegosaurus was represented in the popular Transformers toy line and animated series as Snarl, an Autobot that could transform into a Stegosaurus form. The US state of Colorado lists the Stegosaurus as its state dinosaur.

DID YOU KNOW?

The name 'Stegosaurus' comes from the Greek words 'stegos' meaning roof and 'sauros' meaning lizard. The Stegosaurus was alive in the late Jurassic Period (around 150 million years ago). Stegosaurus fossils have been found in western North America and more recently in Portugal, indicating that they lived in Europe as well.

WOW, REALLY!

In terms of size, the Stegosaurus was large and heavily built. On average, a fully grown Stegosaurus was around 30 ft (9 m) in length, 4 m (14 ft) in height and up to nearly 5 tons in weight. Although the Stegosaurus, body was large, the size of its brain was only around the size of a dog's.

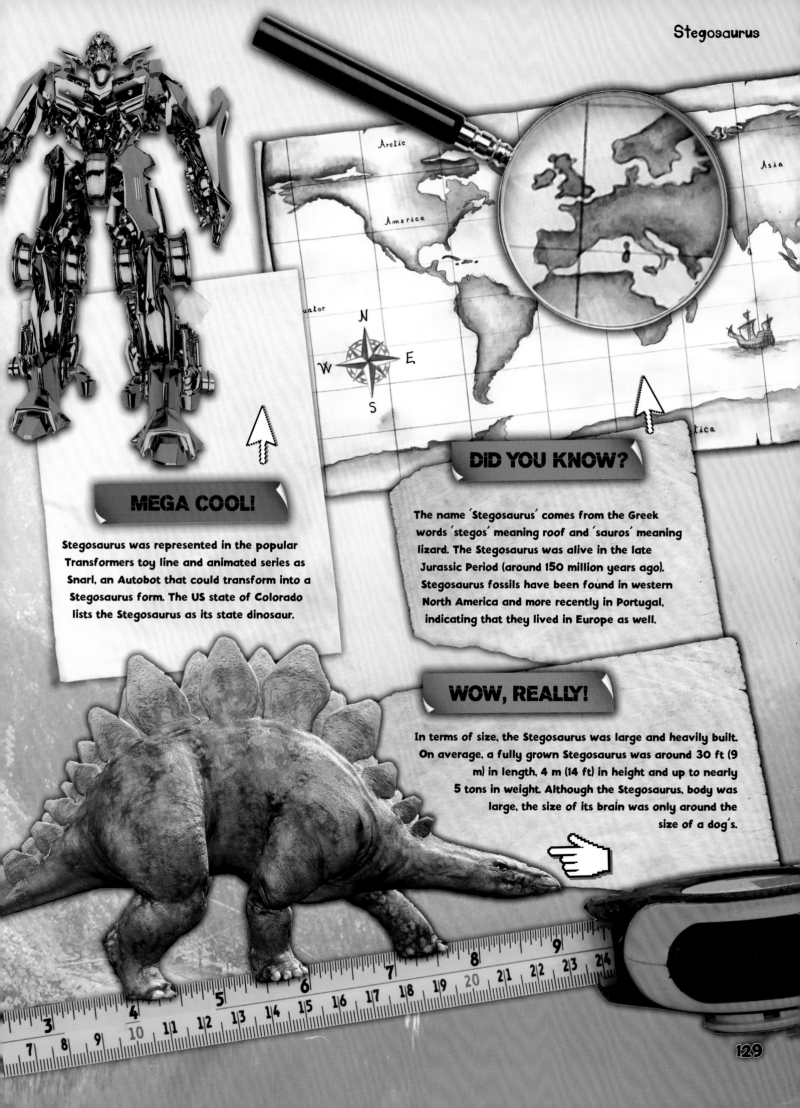

ANKYLOSAURUS

Ankylosaurus was a massive armored dinosaur that lived in the Cretaceous period. It measured about 25-35 ft or 7.5-10.7 m long, it was 6 ft or 1.8 m wide and would have weighed roughly 3-4 tons.

Its armor was really impressive, its back, sides and tail were completely protected. Even its eyelids had plates of bone! In addition to the armor, they had rows of bony spikes that projected from their flanks and bony knobs on its back. Only its tummy was unarmored, so flipping it over was the only way it could be wounded.

NOT THAT BRIGHT!

As big as Ankylosaurus was it had an unusually small brain. It was about the same size as Stegosaurus', which wasn't the brightest of dinosaurs!

DID YOU KNOW?

Ankylosaurus was the Cretaceous equivalent of an armored truck, low-slung, very wide and covered with very thick, almost impenetrable armor.

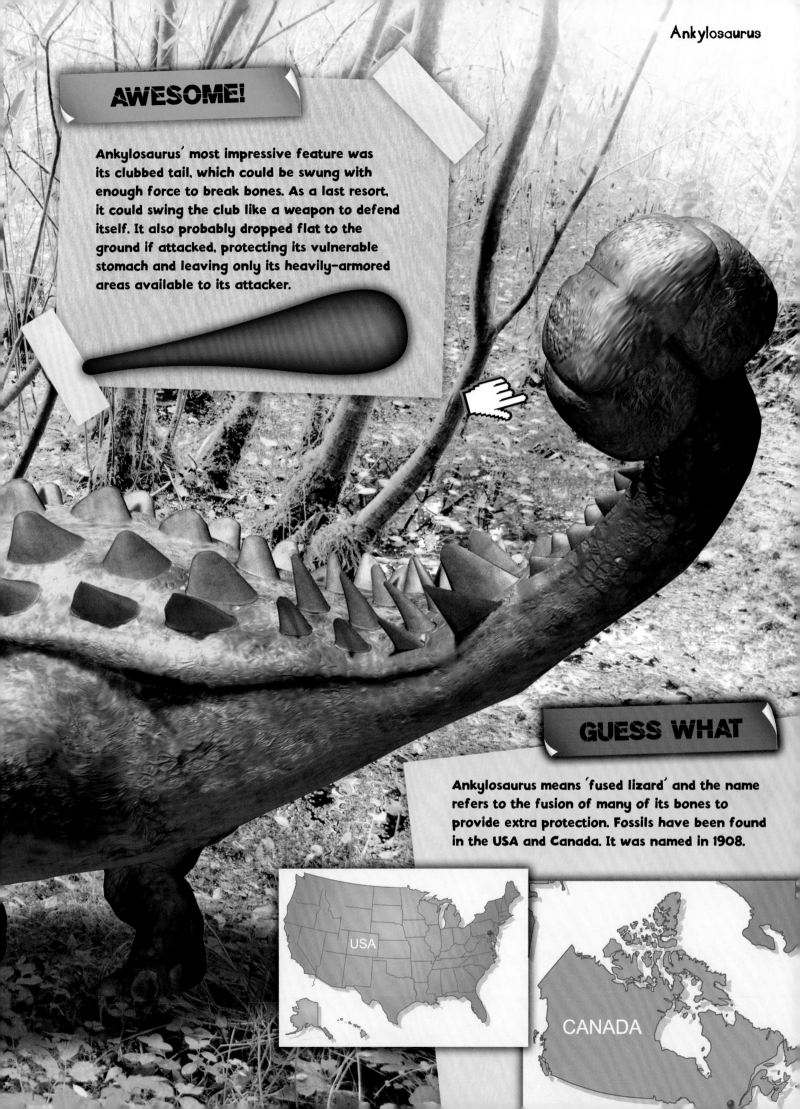

AWESOME!

Ankylosaurus' most impressive feature was its clubbed tail, which could be swung with enough force to break bones. As a last resort, it could swing the club like a weapon to defend itself. It also probably dropped flat to the ground if attacked, protecting its vulnerable stomach and leaving only its heavily-armored areas available to its attacker.

GUESS WHAT

Ankylosaurus means 'fused lizard' and the name refers to the fusion of many of its bones to provide extra protection. Fossils have been found in the USA and Canada. It was named in 1908.

USA

CANADA

KENTROSAURUS

Kentrosaurus means 'spiked lizard' and was named after the dramatic double row of bony spikes that ran from halfway down its back. It lived during the late Jurassic Period, about 156 to 150 million years ago. It had a tiny, narrow head ending with a toothless beak. Small teeth further back in its cheeks helped it to mash up the fern and lush riverside plants it grazed on. There is strong evidence that Kentrosaurus moved and lived in herds.

TWO BRAINS?!

Kentrosaurus was once believed to have two brains! Scientists now know that the second was merely a nerve cluster, which controlled the tail and hind legs.

HOW DO YOU SAY MY NAME?

ken-troh-sawr-us

DID YOU KNOW?

It grew to between 8 ft or 2.5 m long and would have weighed almost two tons. Each of the spikes on Kentrosaurus's back were around 12 in or 30 cm high.

WOW FACT

Kentrosaurus' olfactory bulbs (the area of the brain controlling smell) were very well-developed, so it had a keen sense of smell.

Its back legs were twice as long as its front legs, and it may have been able to stand up for short periods of time just on its back legs, to reach higher-up vegetation such as leaves.

EDMONTONIA

Edmontonia means 'from Edmonton' the place where it was found close to the Edmonton rock formation in Alberta, Canada. It was named in 1928 by C. M. Sternberg. It was an ankylosaur, one of a group of armored plant eaters that lived 76–68 million years ago in the Cretaceous Period. It had scutes (bony plates) on its back and head and sharp spikes along its back and tail. Four large spikes stuck out from its shoulders on each side.

WOW BIG

Edmontonia was one of the largest nodosaurids at 20–23 ft or 6–7 m in length and weighed in at around 3.5 tons.

LIKE A HELMET

Edmontonia's head was covered in armored scales to protect the brain, and two collars of flat bony plates protected the back of the neck.

WOW FACT

Edmontonia had specially arranged shoulder muscles that let it draw in its front legs if it was attacked, allowing it to hold its body close to the ground.

YOU'RE NOT EATING ME!

Slow-moving Edmontonia would have needed every bit of its impressive armor, as it shared time and territory with Tyrannosaurus Rex!

DID YOU KNOW?

Edmontonia had very wide feet which it would have needed in the mostly low-lying coastal areas it lived in, to walk safely around on wet and marshy ground.

SCELIDOSAURUS

Scelidosaurus pronounced skel-eye-doh-SAWR-us and meaning 'limb lizard' was named by Sir Richard Owen in 1859. It lived in the early Jurassic Period around 206 to 200 million years ago. Scelidosaurus was a low-slung, armored, plant-eating dinosaur, with a small head, stocky legs and a long stiffened tail. Its neck was long compared to other armored dinosaurs.

ANKYLOSAUR OR STEGOSAUR?

Scelidosaurus has been classified at different times as a stegosaur or an ankylosaur. The bony plates in its skin resemble a later ankylosaur however the bony plates down its back and heavy body are similar to a stegosaur. So scientists still do not wholly agree about which group it belongs to! It is thought Scelidosaurus might well have been an ancestor to both.

WOW FACT

Its narrow beak contained small leaf-shaped teeth in the front of the upper jaw, useful for slicing flowers and fruits off plants rather than for chewing food.

EXTRA LUNCH!

Young Scelidosaurs may have added extra protein to their diet by eating insects.

DID YOU KNOW?

Scelidosaurus was one of the first of the armored dinosaurs. It was around 10-13 ft or 3-4 m long and weighed about 440-550 lbs or 200-250 kg.

137

SCUTELLOSAURUS

Scutellosaurus means 'little shield lizard' and gets its name from the bony armor 'shields' called scutes that cover its tiny body. It was named by Edwin Colbert in 1981. Scutellosaurus was a plant-eater and spent much of its time grazing. Its hind legs were much longer than its front ones, and scientists believe it probably walked most of the time on four legs, but if attacked it could rise up onto its back legs and run away at a decent speed.

WOW, REALLY

When we think of dinosaurs, especially armored ones, we tend to think of massive creatures but Scutellosaurus weighed no more than a medium sized dog, around 22 lbs or 10 kg!

LONG TAIL!

Scutellosaurs had a short skull. Its tail, on the other hand, was twice the length of its body and head put together.

TWO OR FOUR LEGS?

Scutellosaurus was a creature that could walk on both two and four legs and this is called semi-bipedal (put in bold). Its own ancestors had been fully bipedal and its descendants would be quadrupeds.

DID YOU KNOW?

More than 300 scutes protected Scutellosaurus, these ran along its back and tail. Six different types of bony plates have been found, the largest of which would have formed one or two rows down the center of its back. Any predator trying to take a bite out of this little guy would have been in for a shock!

GUESS WHAT?

Fossils have been found in Arizona, North America but little is really known about this dinosaur as only two incomplete skeletons have been found.

NODOSAURUS

Nodosaurus means 'knobbed or node lizard' and it takes its name from the bony armor plates and knobs which covered most of its skin. It lived during the Cretaceous Period around 110 million years ago. It gave its name to the group of ankylosaurs called nodosaurids. Nodosaurids differ from the other types of ankylosaur in lacking a club at the end of their tail. Nodosaurids were distinguished by the bands of spikes that ran along the sides of their body, pear-shaped heads, and relatively narrow toothless beaks. It was a plant-eater and may have also swallowed small stones to aid grinding up food in its large gut.

NOT THE CLEVEREST!

Nodosarus had a small head and miniscule brain compared to the size of its body, indicating very low intelligence.

GUESS WHAT

Nodosaurus, pronounced Noh-doh-sawr-us, was one of the earliest armored dinosaurs discovered. It was first identified by Othniel Charles Marsh who discovered parts of it in 1889. Fossils have been found in Kansas and Wyoming, North America.

140

DID YOU KNOW?

Nodosaurus was similar to a modern day rhinoceros in that it spent its life moving slowly through the grasslands grazing for food.

ARMOR ITS ONLY DEFENCE!

Nodosaurus had little means of attacking an enemy. If attacked, it probably relied on crouching low to the ground to protect its soft underside.

MINMI

Minmi was an unusually small and primitive armored ankylosaur that walked on four short legs. It had a short neck and a wide skull with a tiny brain and a long tail. A plant-eater, it lived during the early Cretaceous Period, about 119–113 million years ago and would have eaten the low-growing plants of the floodplains and woodlands where it roamed.

Minmi had extra bony plates added to its backbone. These strengthened its back, helping support the weight of its armor. Extra muscles attached to these extra plates could have allowed Minmi to run at a reasonable speed.

WOW FACT

Minmi was about 10 ft or 3 m long and was roughly 3 ft or 1 m tall to the top of the shoulder. It would have been roughly the same size as a year-old calf.

COOL!

Minmi had skin armored with large bony plates and smaller pea-sized bones called ossicles embedded all over it. Even Minmi's underbelly was protected by small bony plates, which makes it unique among the thyreophoran suborder of dinosaurs.

WHAT'S IN A NAME!

Minmi has the shortest name ever given to a dinosaur. Minmi pronounced MIN-mee was name after Minmi Crossing in Australia.

BONZA!

Minmi was the first armored dinosaur found south of the equator. It is also the most complete dinosaur skeleton ever found in Australia. The first fossils were discovered by Alan Batholomai near Roma, Queensland in 1964.

BONE MYSTERY

Minmi was the only ankylosaur to have paravertebrae. Some scientists have suggested that these are actually tendons which have ossified (changed into bone) rather than true bones.

PANOPLOSAURUS

Panoplosaurus was named in 1919 and lived during the late Cretaceous Period around 70 million years ago. It was a plant-eater and had small, simple chewing teeth that were set into a curving jaw, with fleshy cheek pouches for gathering the plants which it ate.

Panoplosaurus had thick bony armor covering much of its body with side-facing spikes protruding from its shoulders and forward-facing spokes from its neck. Its low, heavy, stumpy legs would have been covered with thick scaly hide.

GUESS WHAT

Panoplosaurus, like other armored dinosaurs, would have been virtually immune from being eaten by the hungry raptors and tyrannosaurs that lived during the late Cretaceous in North America.

DID YOU KNOW?

Panoplosaurus fossils have been found in Canada and the USA.

HUAYANGOSAURUS

Huayangosaurus was a small primitive stegosaur, found in East Asia. It belonged to the stegosaur family and had pairs of plates all the way down its back and spikes on its tail. Outward-facing spikes above its hips or shoulders would have helped to protect it from attack.

DID YOU KNOW?

Huayangosaurus lived in the Late Jurassic Period around 165 million years ago which is very interesting, as this is 20 million years before the best-known stegosaur, the North American Stegosaurus.

DINO DATA

PRONUNCIATION: Hoo-ah-yang-oh-sore-us
DIET: Plant eater
HEIGHT: 13 ft or 4 m
WEIGHT: 880 lbs or 400 kg

TITLE

Huayangosaurus was discovered by Dong Zhiming, a famous Chinese paleontologist, and it was named after the place where it was found in 1982.

EGGS AND LIFE CYCLE

Dinosaur eggs were hard-shelled eggs, much like those of reptiles and birds today, laid by the females. They came in a variety of shapes and sizes, some as big as 24 inches or 60 cm long. Even the biggest dinosaurs would have laid small eggs, as the shell needed to be thin enough to allow oxygen in and to allow the baby to get out. Some dinosaurs would have cared for their young but others would have abandoned them as soon as they were born. Very little is known about the family lifestyle of dinosaurs, although some evidence found in the Gobi Desert in the 1920s showed tracks of adults and babies moving together.

NESTS

Dinosaurs scraped nests in the ground, these ranged from simple pits dug into the earth to more elaborately designed nests with mud rims. They sometimes, depending on the species of dinosaur, appeared in large nesting grounds and other times on their own.

FIRST EGG!

The first fossilized dinosaur egg was found in France in 1869 and was laid by Hypselosaurus, a member of the Titanosaurus family.

HOW ON EARTH!

One of the big unanswered questions about dinosaur eggs is how the giant sauropods like Apatosaurus and Diplodocus laid their eggs without breaking them! Given the massive size of these creatures and even if they squatted while laying their eggs, the eggs would have still dropped from a height of roughly 8 ft or 2.5 m and would have been unlikely to survive. Some scientists have argued they may have had a tube that extended for laying eggs, like some modern-day turtles have.

WOW FACT

Dinosaurs appeared to have a homing instinct like a pigeon or swallow, that would guide them back year after year to the same breeding grounds.

DID YOU KNOW?

More than 200 dinosaur egg sites have been found around the world.

147

FLYING DINOSAURS

These next pages explore the dinosaurs with wings.

INTRODUCING ...

DIMORPHODON

CAUDIPTERYX

ARCHAEOPTERYX

PTERANODON

HESPERORNIS

RHAMPHORHYNCHUS

PTEROSAUR

QUETZALCOATLUS

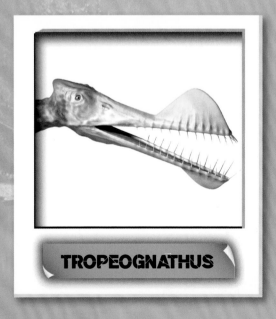

TROPEOGNATHUS

DIMORPHODON

Dimorphodon is one of the earliest primitive flying reptiles that has been discovered. This kind of reptile is called a 'Pterosaur' and lived at the same time as the dinosaurs.

Dimorphodon means 'two-form teeth' due to the fact that it had two distinct types of teeth in its jaw, which is rare among reptiles. The teeth at the front are longer than those at the back.

It had a wingspan of about 6 ft or 1.7 m and it flew well using large, light-weight wings. Its long, thin tail with a diamond-shaped flap of skin at the end helped stabilize it in flight.

WOW REALLY!

It had a huge head which was extremely large compared to the rest of the body, and it is thought the large beak may have been colored, making it useful for display to other Dimorphodons.

DID YOU KNOW?

The first fossils were found in England by fossil collector Mary Anning in December 1828.

GUESS WHAT?

Unlike most other pterosaurs, Dimorphodon had legs which stuck out to the sides, these would have given it a somewhat clumsy, waddling gait.

HOW DO YOU SAY MY NAME?

Die-morf-oh-don

COOL!

Paleontologists suggest that it would have been able to run very fast, rising up onto its toes to do so.

151

CAUDIPTERYX

Caudipteryx has an interesting mix of reptile and bird-like anatomical shapes. It was a small **bipedal** dinosaur, with long legs that would have made it a very fast runner. Its teeth were long, sharp, and had deep, bulbous roots.

Its name means 'tail feather' and refers to this dinosaur's short feathered tail plume.

It was covered in short feathers on its arms and tail, its arms looked like small wings rather than arms but it could not fly. Its long legs and relatively light weight would have made it a very fast runner. Caudipteryx's feathers were useful to warm its eggs, to attract a mate and also provided excellent insulation.

WOW REALLY?

Some scientists think that Caudipteryx proves that birds descended from dinosaurs. Its feathers suggest that it might be the missing link in the evolution of birds from dinosaurs.

DID YOU KNOW?

Caudipteryx was around 3 ft or 1 m long and weighed in at about 20 pounds (9 kg) – that's the same weight as a turkey!

GUESS WHAT?

Philip Currie identified the fossils in 1997 in China.

COOL!

Caudipteryx's teeth faced outwards, giving it a distinctly buck-toothed appearance. It is possible it had a diet consisting of plants, small fish and other small animals.

153

ARCHAEOPTERYX

Archaeopteryx means 'ancient feather', it was named by Hermann von Meyer in 1861. It lived in the Jurassic Period around 150 million years ago. It had a small head, long neck, compact body, and a fan of tail feathers. It also had the bone structure of a dinosaur, while it appeared to be a bird.

WOW REALLY?

Its inner ear was very similar to a bird, and the areas controlling movement and vision were enlarged, that's why we can say that Archaeopteryx's brain was designed for flight and balance!

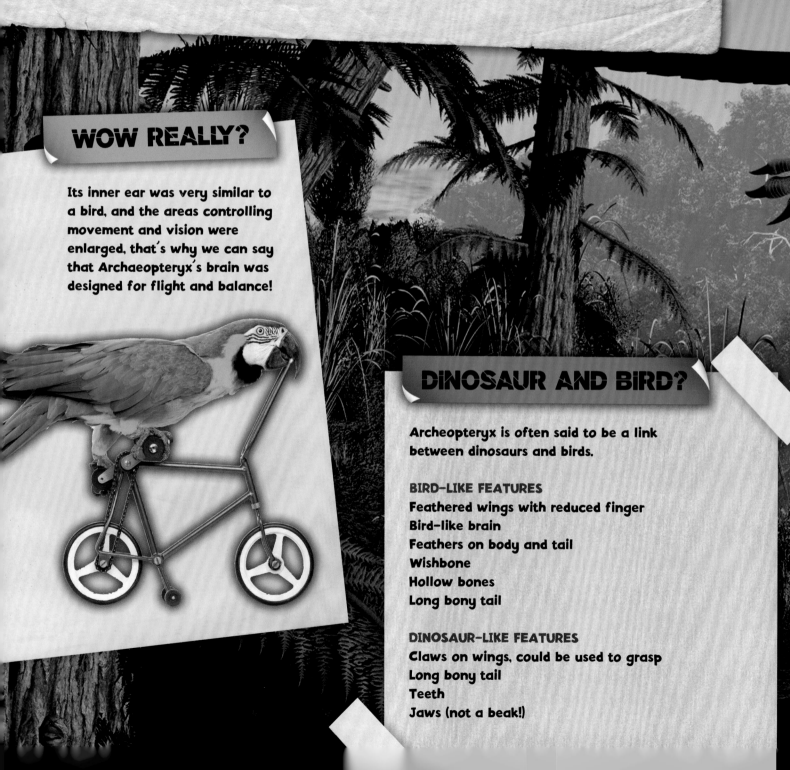

DINOSAUR AND BIRD?

Archeopteryx is often said to be a link between dinosaurs and birds.

BIRD-LIKE FEATURES
Feathered wings with reduced finger
Bird-like brain
Feathers on body and tail
Wishbone
Hollow bones
Long bony tail

DINOSAUR-LIKE FEATURES
Claws on wings, could be used to grasp
Long bony tail
Teeth
Jaws (not a beak!)

DID YOU KNOW?

It had large eyes which would have given it excellent vision.

GUESS WHAT?

Scientists have argued over whether or not this animal could fly, ever since the first Archaeopteryx fossil was found. Studies into an Achaeopteryx's brain by Dr Angela Milner, have led to the belief that it did fly but not very well!

PTERANODON

Pteranodon was a massive flying reptile that lived near the coast during the Cretaceous Period, it was not a true dinosaur but was related to them. Even though it had no teeth, it was carnivorous and had excellent eyesight and a scoop-like beak which would have helped it to catch fish straight from the surface of the water. The fact that fossil skeletons where found near the sea lets us know that fish were an important part of its diet.

WOW REALLY?

Pteranodon would have been agile, elegant and quite fast when flying, reaching speeds up to 30 mph (48 kph).

MPH

60 80
40 100
20
120
0
000108 140

HOW DO YOU SAY MY NAME?

Ter-an-o-don

DID YOU KNOW?

Pteranodon's lower jaw was over 3 feet or 1 meter in length. It had a wing span of up to 30-33 ft or 9-10 m and it would have weighed around 44-55 lbs or 20-25 kg.

COOL!

It probably looked more like a giant bat than a bird with large, soft, hair-covered membranes for wings which were very thin but extremely strong. This reptile didn't have any feathers.

WALKED AND FLEW!

Pteranodon would have been able to walk on the ground but once in the air would have looked like a huge glider. It would have been able to fly long distances using its light-weight wings.

GUESS WHAT?

Pteranodon had a long head crest that was probably used to help counter balance the weight of its massive beak.

HESPERORNIS

Hesperornis was a large bird, reaching up to 6 ft (1.8 m) in length. It had virtually no wings, and swam with its powerful hind legs. It belongs to a group of dinosaurs called the Hesperornithifornis. It was a dinosaur that lived in the sea during the Cretaceous Period. Its name means 'Western bird' and was named by paleontologist Othniel C. Marsh in 1871. It was a very important discovery because it filled a big gap in the fossil history of birds. Hesperornis had teeth as well as a beak, which were used to hold prey.

A talented swimmer and diver, Hesperornis spent its day cooling in the sea breeze and hunting fish and other sea animals. On land, it was awkward and clumsy. It would have moved by sliding about on its belly due to the position of its hip bones and back legs.

WOW, REALLY

Hesperornis was about the size of a full-grown human.

SWIM FOR YOUR LIFE!

Unable to fly or walk, Hesperornis was in danger from predators both in the water and on land – good job it was a fast swimmer!

HOW DO YOU SAY MY NAME?

Hes-per-or-nis.

DID YOU KNOW?

They were the only true marine dinosaurs of the whole Mesozoic Era and Hesperornis was one of the largest birds to have lived during the age of the dinosaurs.

GUESS WHAT?

Unlike modern flightless penguins, it did not use its wings as well as its feet to push itself through the water. Its wings were tiny and of no use, but its back iegs were powerful.

RHAMPHORHYNCHUS

Rhamphorhynchus means 'beak snout', and it was a pterosaur which lived during the late Jurassic Period. It had a long tail, stiffened with ligaments, and a wingspan up to 6 ft or 1.75 m.

Rhamphorhynchus fed by dipping its head into the lakes and rivers of late Jurassic Europe and scooping up wriggling fish thanks to its narrow beak and sharp teeth. Due to the fact that it had tiny legs Rhamphorhynchus wouldn't have hunted on land, because it would have been a poor runner.

It had a long, thin and pointed tail, which helped with its balance in flight.

WOW REALLY?

Rhamphorhynchus had thin, long jaws with amazingly sharp teeth. It is believed that it hunted by dragging its beak in the water in the hope of coming into contact with fish, then it would snap its needle-sharp teeth shut and toss the food into its throat pouch.

HOW DO YOU SAY MY NAME?

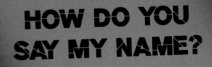

Ram-for-ink-us

COOL!

At the end of its tail it had a flap of skin, which was the shape of a diamond.

DID YOU KNOW?

This pterosaur was less than 1 foot (30 cm) long, but its wings, when fully extended, stretched for a distance of 3 feet (90 cm) from tip to tip.

GUESS WHAT?

Rhamphorhynchus fossils have been recovered from Jurassic marine clays in southern England and Portugal but the finest specimens come from the Solnhofen quarry in Bavaria, southern Germany.

PTEROSAUR

Pterosaur means 'winged lizard', and it was a flying reptile that lived from the late Triassic Period to the end of the Cretaceous, 228 to 65 million years ago. The evidence for flight comes from their light hollow bones, large brains and an extremely long fourth digit providing wing support. Pterosaurs had hair, as shown by the fossils and so had to have been warm-blooded. They would have lived on a diet of fish, molluscs and insects.

WOW REALLY?

Pterosaur had a large brain and good eyesight.

DID YOU KNOW?

Its wings were covered with a leathery and tough membrane that stretched between its body, the top of its legs and its fourth finger.

WRONG DINO!

Not all Pterosaurs are the same.
There were many different types of
Pterosaurs and their wing designs
differed. This meant that some of
the species flapped their wings
and could fly with great power.
Others simply glided through the air,
relying on updrafts of warm air to
help them fly.

IT IS A DUCK OR A BIRD?

When Pterosaurs were first
discovered it was thought that
they lived in water, possibly
because some species had
webbed feet. However in the
19th century George Cuvier
proposed that Pterosaurs flew.

EXTRA LUNCH!

Young Pterosaurs may have
added extra protein to their diet
by eating insects.

QUETZALCOATLUS

Quetzalcoatlus was one of the largest flying animals to have ever lived on Earth. It was a member of a family of advanced toothless pterosaurs with unusually long necks. Its slender jaws were toothless and its head was topped by a long, bony crest. At the front of its wings there were three-fingered hands which had sharp claws. As with birds today its hollow bones would have helped it to fly and remain airborne despite its vast size.

Quetzalcoatlus was named after the Aztec feathered serpent god in 1975. It lived at the same time as Triceratops and Tyrannosaurus Rex. Quetzalcoatlus became extinct at the end of the Cretaceous Period 65 million years ago.

WOW REALLY?

It had the same weight as an adult human with a weight of around 154 lbs or 70 kg.

HOW DO YOU SAY MY NAME?

Kett-zal-coe-at-luss

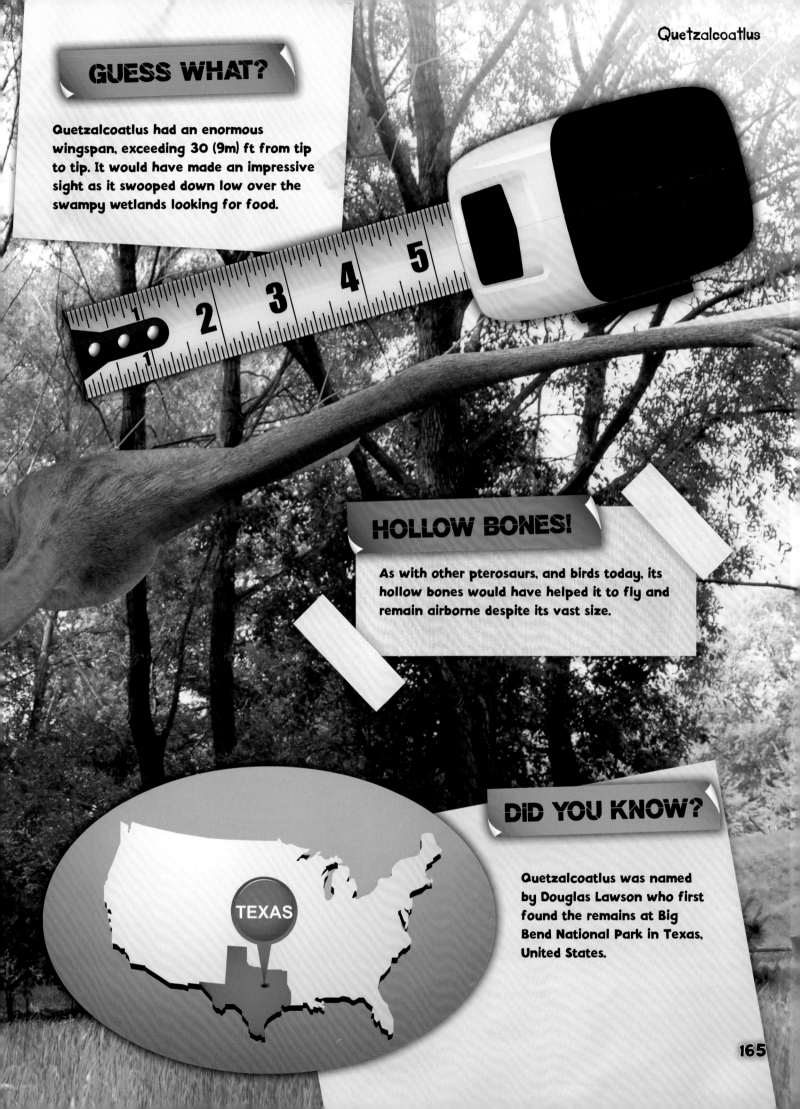

GUESS WHAT?

Quetzalcoatlus had an enormous wingspan, exceeding 30 (9m) ft from tip to tip. It would have made an impressive sight as it swooped down low over the swampy wetlands looking for food.

HOLLOW BONES!

As with other pterosaurs, and birds today, its hollow bones would have helped it to fly and remain airborne despite its vast size.

DID YOU KNOW?

Quetzalcoatlus was named by Douglas Lawson who first found the remains at Big Bend National Park in Texas, United States.

TEXAS

TROPEOGNATHUS

Tropeognathus lived near coastal waters during the Cretaceous Period where it hunted fish and other animals living in the shallow waters. Its weight was around 26-31 lb (12-14 kg) which made it light enough to prey on fish and squid at the surface of lakes and swamps. It had around 48 teeth in total for catching, killing and eating. While it was catching its prey, the dinosaur used its crest bone to stabilize the head.

Paleontologists believe Tropeognathus would travel many miles searching for food, using warm thermals to take off and soar through the air.

WOW REALLY?

Tropeognathus was very large, its wingspan was nearly 20 feet or 6m wide.

GUESS WHAT?

Tropeognathus had large bumps on the top and bottom of its beak. Scientists believe that this may have helped Tropeognathus remain stable as it flew over the water, dragging its beak under the surface.

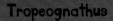

COOL!

It could feed like a flamingo trailing its beak in the water.

DID YOU KNOW?

Tropeognathus fossils were discovered in rocks in the Santana Formation in north eastern Brazil and have been very precisely dated to 115 million years ago.

YOU CAN'T CATCH ME!

It tended to remain near water, resting on cliffs as it went but rarely venturing very far inland where it might get hunted.

HORNED DINOSAURS

Here we find out about some of the scariest looking dinosaurs, one in particular was mistaken for the devil when it was first found! With their long horns, you wouldn't want to meet this lot on a dark night!

INTRODUCING ...

TRICERATOPS

PROTOCERATOPS

ARRHINOCERATOPS

MICROCERATOPS

LEPTOCERATOPS

STYGIMOLOCH

CENTROSAURUS

STYRACOSAURUS

PSITTACOSAURUS

TRICERATOPS

Triceratops is one of the most famous of all the dinosaurs. It lived in what is now North America in the late Cretaceous Period, about 72 to 65 million years ago, toward the end of the Mesozoic Era, the Age of Reptiles. It was among the last of the dinosaur species to evolve before the Cretaceous-Tertiary extinction. Triceratops was a plant-eater and probably used its powerful beak to crush food, such as vegetation. It probably ate cycads and other low-lying plants with its tough beak. Triceratops walked on four short legs and would have been a relatively slow dinosaur.

WOW BIG HEAD!

Triceratops had one of the largest skulls of any land animal discovered so far, some skulls measured a massive 10 ft or 3 m in length.

WOW FACT!

Although the name Triceratops means 'three-horned face,' not all specimens had three horns. Often the nasal horn was either very short or nearly absent. However, the two brow horns, which grew out of the top of the skull over each eye, were always large and well developed.

MEGA BUCKS!

One reason Triceratops is so well known is because of its large, bony skull, which fossilized fairly easily and often in one piece. For this reason, complete Triceratops skulls have become prized items at auctions worldwide, fetching millions of dollars from wealthy bidders. The most famous recent example is Triceratops Cliff, purchased for $1 million in 2008 by a wealthy dinosaur fan and donated to the Boston Museum of Science.

WOW MISTAKE!

The paleontologist who named Triceratops thought it was an ancient bison. In 1887, the famous palaeontologist Othniel C. Marsh examined a Triceratops' skull, complete with horns, and assigned the remains to the grazing mammal *Bison alticornis*, which didn't evolve until tens of millions of years later. Fortunately for his reputation, Marsh quickly reversed the error.

PROTOCERATOPS

Protoceratops means 'before the horned faces' and it lived in the scrublands and deserts of Asia in the Late Cretaceous Period around 85-70 million years ago. It was a plant-eater and it probably ate cycads and other prehistoric plants with its tough, hook-like beak. Protoceratops walked on four legs, had a large head, a bulky body, a parrot-like beak, cheek teeth, and a small frill on its head. Protoceratops lacked any well-developed horns, however it did have thick bumps of bone on its nose and small bumps above its eyes, exactly where later horned dinosaurs would have had their horns.

DID YOU KNOW?

Whenever paleontologists discover multiple fossils of a dinosaur genus in any given location, the most logical conclusion (usually) is that this creature roamed in packs or herds. It's likely that Protoceratops traveled in herds of hundreds, and perhaps even thousands, of individuals.

HOW DO YOU SAY MY NAME?

Pro-toe-serr-a-tops

NOT AS BIG AS YOU THINK!

Protoceratops is one of those dinosaurs that people think was a lot bigger than it actually was: today, it's often mistakenly pictured as a giant, but this horned dinosaur was only about 6 ft or 2 m in length and 30 in or 75 cm high. The recorded weights for Protoceratops vary but it is thought be around 880 lbs or 400 kg.

WOW FAMOUS!

Protoceratops has earned a place in the paleontology hall of fame for a rare fossil find, in 1971 in the Gobi Desert: The tangled skeletons of a Protoceratops and a Velociraptor, who were thought to be in mid-fight when they were both buried together by a sudden sandstorm, preserving their battle forever!

ARRHINOCERATOPS

Arrhinoceratops was a plant-eating dinosaur that lived in the woodlands of North America in the late Cretaceous Period around 70-65 million years ago. Arrhinoceratops stood a massive 20 ft or 6 m off the ground and with its outward pointing horns and large neck frill, it would have looked really big and scary. Arrhinoceratops are believed to have lived and travelled around in herds. This is because paleontologists found groups of fossils together. They would have fed from vegetation as they traveled together and probably ate ferns, cycads and pine needles. If attacked, Arrhinoceratops could have defended itself with a sharp peck from its parrot-like beak.

HOW DO YOU SAY MY NAME?

Ay-rye-no-serra-tops.

WOW FACT

Arrhinoceratops' neck frill had holes in the bone which are called fenestrae (windows). This made the bone lighter so that its head was not impossibly heavy to hold up.

HORN OR NO HORN?

When its fossil was first discovered, in Alberta, Canada in 1923 by W.A. Parks, Arrhinoceratops seemed to be missing the small nose horn possessed by most ceratopsians – hence its name, Greek for 'no-nose horned face'. However later investigations showed Arrhinoceratops had a horn after all, making it a very close cousin of Triceratops and Torosaurus. Arrhinoceratops lived alongside other horned dinosaurs in North America where it foraged for plant life to eat. Arrhinoceratops used its sharp parrot-like beak to cut through this plant material.

MICROCERATOPS/ MICROCERATUS

Microceratops, pronounced mike-roe-seh-rah-tops, means 'small horned face' is the smallest known horned dinosaur. A plant-eater, it lived in Asia around 70 million years ago in the Late Cretaceous Period. Microceratops was around 30 in or 76 cm long and 24 in or 60 cm high and was both small and lightly built. This probably made Microceratops very agile and fast. Microceratops' back legs were longer than its front legs, allowing it to balance and hop on the hind legs when needed. Information about Microceratops is based on very limited fossil remains, so there's still a lot we don't know about this dinosaur.

Microceratops did not have any horns, but it did have the obvious head frill so common with horned dinosaurs.

DID YOU KNOW?

Microceratops received a name change in 2008, to the slightly less catchy Microceratus. The reason for the change is that, unknown to the dinosaur palaeontology community, the name Microceratops had already been assigned to a genus of wasp, and the classification rules say that no two creatures, no matter how different, can have the same genus name.

WHERE WAS MICROCERATOPS FOUND?

Microceratops was discovered in 1953 in Mongolia. Subsequently, additional fossils have been found in Mongolia and also in China.

SMALL BUT NOT THAT SMALL!

Microceratops was not quite the smallest dinosaur that ever lived – that was compsognathus longipes, which was only the size of a chicken.

AWESOME!

Microcertatops appeared as part of the herd in the Walt Disney film *Dinosaur* (2000).

177

LEPTOCERATOPS

Leptoceratops lived on the plains of western North America in the Late Cretaceous Period around 70 million years ago, however see our awesome fact for more recent news on new Leptoceratops discoveries. A plant-eater, Leptoceratops had a small head frill, and no horns. They usually walked on all fours, but could also stand and run on two legs. Leptoceratops' front digits had the ability to grasp, and were probably used to pull branches and other food towards its mouth. It would also have used it's sharp, parrot-shaped beak to slice off leaves. Leptoceratops was around 8 ft or 2.4 m long.

LOOK AFTER THOSE TEETH!

Leptoceratops' teeth were different to those of its fellow ceratopsians. They were broad instead of long, which may have helped it chew up all kinds of different vegetation. They had single roots, and each tooth had only one replacement tooth available – most ceratopsians had several teeth ready to take the place of one that was broken or fell out.

DiD YOU KNOW?

Leptoceratops was discovered in 1924 by Barnum Brown in North America. Scientists believe that Leptoceratops was a late-surviving primitive horned dinosaur. More recently fossilized Leptoceratops bones have been found in Australia, showing that they may have lived all over the world.

AWESOME

The fossil finds in Australia also date from the early Cretaceous Period, whereas all previous finds dated from towards the end of the period. It seems Leptoceratops may have walked the earth for some 50 million years!

STYGIMOLOCH

Stygimoloch was discovered in Hell Creek, Montana, in the 1800s. Its finders thought it resembled a demon, although this dinosaur was a herbivore that grazed the woodlands of North America, 74–65 million years ago. Stygimoloch did have an unusually large head with bony protuberances, a whole collection of horns, some as long as 4 in or 10 cm. It was a small dinosaur, around 6.5–10 ft (2–3 m) long and most likely weighed around 220 lbs or 100 kg. It probably lived in herds.

WOW SCAREY!

In Greek myth, the River Styx flowed through the underworld called Hades (Hell). However Stygimoloch wasn't nearly as terrifying as its name implies. A type of pachycephalosaur, or bone-headed dinosaur, it was actually fairly lightweight, about the size of a fully grown man. It earned its intimidating name because its skull evoked the Christian concept of the devil, all horns and scales, with the slight hint of an evil leer.

FAMOUS!

The first appearance of Stygimoloch in a film was in the Disney movie *Dinosaur* in 2000.

NEW INFORMATION!

The 1995 discovery of a Stygimoloch skeleton cast doubt on the long-held belief that it butted heads like a goat with other herd members. If it had done this, it would probably have broken its neck!

HOW DO YOU SAY MY NAME?

Stig-ih-moe-lock.

DID YOU KNOW?

The first complete Stygimoloch skeleton was not found until 1995, it was discovered by fossil hunter Mike Triebold.

CENTROSAURUS

Centrosaurus means 'sharp pointed lizard' and is pronounced SEN-tro-SORE-us. Centrosaurus was a four-legged plant-eating dinosaur that had many horns on its head. Centrosaurus lived in herds during the late Cretaceous Period, roughly 85 million years ago in the woodlands of western North America. Centosaur was about 20 ft or 6 m long, 6 ft or 1.8 m tall, and would have weighed about 3 tons. It had short powerful legs that ended in feet with five toes. Each toe had a short claw and the foot had developed, hoofed pads. Centrosaurus was the first of the 'short frilled' ceratops to be discovered.

SCAN ME
Instructions on page 5

IMPRESSIVE HORN!

Centrosaurus' most distinctive feature was its impressive horn growing from its nose which was 18 inches or 46 cm long! In different species of Centrosaurus this horn curved either forward or backwards.

DiET

Low lying plants

LOST RELATIVES!

Recently, paleontologists announced a find of a pair of new ceratopsians that seem to have been closely related to Centrosaurus, the North American Diabloceratops and Medusaceratops both of which had unique horn/frill combinations reminiscent of their more famous cousin.

183

STYRACOSAURUS

Styracosaurus meaning 'spiked lizard', had the most impressive set of horns ever seen in the animal kingdom. Six long horns stuck out backwards from its neck frill, it also had a smaller horn above each eye as well as a long horn 2 ft or 60 cm long sticking out from its nose!

Styracosaurus lived in the woodlands of North America in the Late Cretaceous Period around 75-70 million years ago. It was a plant-eater and would have spent its days looking for foliage and also looking out for enemies. If attacked, Styracosaurus could have inflicted great damage on a predator with its horns.

WOW BIG

Styracosaurus was 18 ft or 5.5 m long and around 6 ft or 2 m tall, this is about the size of an elephant and like an elephant it had very tough skin. In spite of its bulk, scientists believe Styracosaurus might have been able to run at up to 20 mph or 32 kph when it needed to. That's the same speed as a car travels in a town.

WOW WHAT A LOT OF FOSSILS!

Styracosaurus most likely lived in herds, moving around their territory slowly in large groups, taking care of their young and feeding. Large deposits of its fossilized bones have been found together in one area. One find was as many as 100 Styracosaurus fossils! The first fossils were found in Alberta in 1913 by Lawrence M Lambe.

PSITTACOSAURUS

Psittacosaurus was among the smallest and first of the Ceratopsia, or horned dinosaurs. It would have only stood about waist high to a full grown human, measured around 6 ft or 2 m long and weighed about 50-175 lbs or 25-80 kg, depending on species. Psittacosaurus lived in the scrublands and deserts of Asia in the early to middle Cretaceous Period around 110 million years ago. Like many other horned dinosaurs, Psittacosaurus was an agile and fast plant-eater, which probably contributed to its long life. Although it is often depicted in a four-legged posture, paleontologists believe some species of Psittacosaurus (there are at least 10 known varieties) walked or ran on two legs. This dinosaur seems to have led a relatively quiet life.

WOW FACT

Psittacosaurus pronounced sih-tack-oh-SORE-us, means 'parrot lizard'. The name comes from this dinosaur's distinctly parrot-shaped beak. It had very few teeth, which were spade-shaped and located at the back of the jaw.

AWESOME

Some Psittacosaurus fossils have been found with preserved impressions of skin – so we know the Psittacosaurus was covered with fine, pebble-like scales, with larger scales over its shoulder area.

WOW TINY

One of the smallest dinosaur fossils ever discovered is that of a baby Psittacosaurus less than 16 in (40 cm) long. New hatchlings would have been even smaller. There's also solid evidence that Psittacosaurus cared for its young after they hatched, like the duck-billed dinosaurs Maiasaura and Hypacrosaurus.

SKELETONS

The study of all dinosaurs starts with the skeletons. Anatomically, dinosaurs have skeletal features which help scientists to identify them as dinosaurs. Most skeletons are discovered from excavated dinosaur fossils. Unless a complete skeleton is found, which is rare, scientists have to reference information from other fossil finds or make an educated guess using scientific software as to what the dinosaur would have looked like.

WHAT MAKES A DINOSAUR A DINOSAUR!

Dinosaurs are classified by their hip structure. This is important because dinosaurs, unlike reptiles whose legs sprawl out to the side, walked with their legs under their bodies. Dinosaurs have two types of hip structure: lizard-hipped and bird-hipped.

Dinosaurs also have a reduced fourth and fifth digit on their hands and their feet have three large toes.

SCAN ME
Instructions on page 5

ALL DINOSAURS ARE NOT THE SAME!

Different shaped dinosaurs have different skeletal structures, for example T-Rex (see page 30) was large and bulky, with a big head and powerful jaws, it only would have been able to move quickly over short distances. However Hypsilophodon (see page 162) had a slimmed down structure, like a gazelle, giving it maximum support but minimum weight so it could run fast over long distances.

SKULL FACT

The shape of a dinosaur's skull, as well as the size, shape and arrangement of its teeth, can tell paleontologists a lot about its diet. The biggest skull ever found belonged to Torosaurus and was 8 foot (2.5m) long.

AWESOME FACT

Skeletons also give scientists an idea of the size of a dinosaur and what it would have looked like. If you stood next to Brachiosaurus' leg you would hardly reach its knees!

COOL FACT!

Sue, the largest and most complete T-Rex skeleton in the world, is on permanent exhibition at The Field Museum in Chicago. Dinosaur Sue even has her own Twitter account @ SUEtheTrex.

DID YOU KNOW

The first near-complete skeleton of a dinosaur was discovered by William Parker Foulke in 1858. It was of a Hadrosaurus.

BIRD-FOOTED DINOSAURS

In this section we meet the bird footed dinosaurs of the Triassic to the Cretaceous Periods, they had short forelimbs and walked or ran on strong hind legs.

INTRODUCING ...

IGUANODON

GALLIMIMUS

DRINKER

LEAELLYNASAURA

CAMPTOSAURUS

HYPSILOPHODON

THESCELOSAURUS

TENONTOSAURUS

OTHNIELIA

ALTIRHINUS

DRYOSAURUS

ORODROMEUS

IGUANODON

Iguanodon was a plant-eating dinosaur that had a conical spike on each thumb. This 30 ft (9 m) dinosaur lived during the early Cretaceous Period, about 135 to 125 million years ago. The supercontinent Pangaea was breaking up at this time, but Iguanodon managed to spread to all the continents except Antarctica.

Iguanodon could run on two legs or walk on four, it was quite a fast dinosaur. It had a flat, stiff tail and three-toed hind feet with hoof-like claws. Its legs were much larger than its arms.

IGUANODON STATS

Iguanodon averaged about
30 ft (9.3 m) long,
16 ft (5 m) tall,
9 ft (2.7 m) tall at the hips,
It may have weighed around 4 to 5 tons.
Iguanodon may have travelled as fast as 9.3–12 mph (15-20 kph)

AWESOME

Iguanodon probably nipped prehistoric plants with its tough, toothed beak. It had no teeth in the front of its mouth, but had strong teeth (about 2 in or 5 cm long) in the side of its jaw which it used to grind up tough plant material. Muscle attachment areas inside its head suggest that it may have had a long tongue.

SUPER FACT

Iguanodon bones have been found on nearly every continent of the world.

WOW FACT

Iguanodon's outstanding feature was a five-fingered hand made up of a spiked thumb used for defence or perhaps foraging, three middle fingers and a fifth finger for grabbing.

DID YOU KNOW?

Iguanodon (pronounced 'Ig-wan-oh-don') was one of the first dinosaurs to be discovered. The name is from 'Iguana' – a type of modern reptile, and 'don' meaning tooth. Iguanodon was named by Gideon A. Mantell in 1825. It's teeth and a few bones were found in 1822 in Sussex, England.

GALLIMIMUS

Gallimimus meaning 'chicken mimic' was the largest of the ornithomimids (the 'ostrich dinosaurs') known. It has been found only in the Late Cretaceous Nemegt Formation of Mongolia and lived about 75-70 million years ago.

Gallimimus was a fast-running dinosaur with a very long, thin, flattened, toothless, horny beak, a small head, and a quite large brain. It had a long neck, long tail, and long legs. Gallimuimum measured around 13-20 ft (4-6 m) long, was 6.3 ft (1.9 m() tall at the hips, and may have weighed about 440 kg (970 lbs). It had large eyes positioned on opposite sides of its head.

DID YOU KNOW?

Gallimimus had short arms with three clawed fingers on each hand, and long legs with three clawed toes. A long tail acted as a counterbalance and kept it upright during fast turns. Its bones were hollow.

WOW SPEEDY!

Gallimimus walked on two long, slender legs. It was a fast, agile dinosaur, probably running about as quickly as an ostrich can run – up to 43 mph (70 kph).

GREEDY

Gallimimus may have been an omnivore, eating small animals like insects and lizards, eggs, and some plant material, by sieving them from mud with comb-like plates in its mouth. The bottom front part of its beak was shaped like a shovel.

193

DRINKER

Drinker lived around 150 million years ago during the Late Jurassic Period, it was a small plant-eating dinosaur and lived near ancient swamps. This herbivore, or plant-eating dinosaur, was only about 6 ft (2 m) long, or about the size of a full grown human man. This is small compared to many other dinosaurs.

Drinker was small as well as agile and walked on two feet. It had unusually broad feet and long, wide-spread toes which may have evolved to negotiate a swampy habitat within Wyoming's Late Jurassic Morrison Formation where fossils were found.

WOW FACT

The palentologist Bob Bakker has reported finding the remains of over 30 Dinker dinosaurs in what might have been a burrow (though, of course, it could have just been a hole!). All known specimens have a floppy tail, this is the tail of choice for negotiating tight tunnel bends.

'THE BONE WAR'

In the late 19th century, Edward Drinker Cope and Othniel C. Marsh were big enemies, trying to get one-up on each other on their paleontological digs, by fair means or foul! They spied, sabotaged and openly slandered each other at every given opportunity! That's why it's ironic that the small, two-legged ornithopod Drinker (named after Cope) may be exactly the same animal as the small, two-legged ornithopod Othnielia (named after Marsh); the differences between these dinosaurs are so minimal that they may one day be collapsed into the same genus.

195

LEAELLYNASAURA

Leaellynasaura was a small, plant-eating dinosaur. It lived during the early Cretaceous Period around 110 million years ago. Leaellynasaura is one of many dinosaurs whose partial remains have been dug (and blasted) out of the solid rocks of Dinosaur Cove in the south east of Australia. A small member of the Ornithopoda group, Leaellynasaura is most notable for its large eyes and large brain.

LEAELLYNASUARA STATS

MEANING:	Leaellynasaura means 'Leaellyn's lizard' – Leaellyn is the daughter of the paleontologists who discovered this dinosaur
PRONOUNCED:	Lee-ell-lin-ah-saw-rah
NAMED BY:	Thomas Rich and Patricia Vickers-Rich
WHEN NAMED:	1989
LENGTH:	6.5–10 ft or 2–3 m long
HEIGHT:	2 ft or 60 cm tall at the hips
WEIGHT:	300 lbs or 135 kg

AWESOME!

Leaellynasuara's tail was three times as long as the rest of the body combined.

WOW FACT

Why were this dinosaur's eyes so large? Scientists have developed a couple of possible theories. Firstly, many believe that it lived deep within thick dark forests where little light could reach the ground. Another theory is that Leaellynasaura would have needed large eyes to see during the long dark winters that were a part of everyday life in Australia at that time. Odd to think of Australia having such winters, but this part of the world fell within the Antarctic circle at this time.

HOW DO YOU SAY MY NAME?

lee-ell-lin-ah-saw-rah

CAMPTOSAURUS

Camptosaurus meaning 'bent lizard' was a plant-eater from the late Jurassic Period and lived around 156 to 145 million years ago. Camptosaurus looked a lot like Iguanodon. It was a heavy dinosaur that was about 16-23 ft (5-7 m) long and 3-4 ft (1m) high at the hips, weighing roughly 2,200 lbs (1000 kg).

It had a long snout, hundreds of teeth and a horny beak. Its legs were longer than its arms and it had four-toed feet and five-fingered arms, all with hooves. It could walk on two or four legs, it probably went on all four to graze for low-lying plants.

DID YOU KNOW?

Camptosaurus was first discovered in 1879 by paleontologist Earl Douglass in Utah, USA. That same year, this new dinosaur was given the name Camptonotus by Othniel Charles Marsh. It was later renamed in 1885 by Marsh because its original name already belonged to a type of cricket.

WHY WAS IT CALLED THAT?

Camptosaurus fed with its short front legs on the ground, and the tall hips and rounded curve of the tail gave it a curved or bent profile. This is why it got its name, which means 'bent reptile.'

AWESOME!

Camptosaurus was one of the earliest ornithopods discovered, it suffered the fate of living with more dinosaurs than could comfortably fit. For this reason, it's now believed that only one identified fossil specimen was a true Camptosaurus; the others may well have been species of Iguanodon (which lived much later, during the Cretaceous Period).

HYPSILOPHODON

Hypsilophodon roamed the Earth during the Early Cretaceous Period, around 140 million years ago, and is considered to have belonged to the Ornithopoda, or bird-footed group. Hypsilophodon measured about 6.5 ft (2 m) long and 2 ft (0.6 m) tall, weighing about 68 kg or 150 lbs. Hypsilophodon had a beak made of horn, cheek pouches and 28–30 self-sharpening cheek teeth in a small skull. Hypsilophodon may have had 2 rows of bony plates running down its back.

Slender legs and a stiffened tail gave it speed and agility. It had large eyes, strong jaws, five-fingered hands and four-toed feet, and one toe on each foot had a hind claw.

DID YOU KNOW?

Hypsilophodon, pronounced Hip-sill-owe-foe-don and meaning 'High-Ridged Teeth', was discovered in 1869 by Gideon Mantall on England's Isle of Wight, or 'Dinosaur Island.' The name Hypsilophodon comes from the shape of its teeth, which allowed it to grind up its food prior to swallowing it. This smaller dinosaur is one of very few reptiles to have had cheeks, a feature that allowed it to keep food stored in its mouth while it chewed, similar to how humans chew food today.

PEOPLE USED TO THINK...

For years scientists believed that Hypsilophodon may have lived in trees. However, this theory is no longer accepted today as accurate.

TINY

Hypsilophodon was one of the smallest dinosaurs.

TWO LEGS

It was bipedal, walking on two feet with only small forelimbs.

THESCELOSAURUS

Thescelosaurus, Greek for 'wonderful lizard' and pronounced thess-keh-low-sore-us, lived in the woodlands of North America in the Late Cretaceous about 70–65 million years ago. Thescelosaurus was about 13 ft or 4 m and weighed around 300 kg or 600 lbs.

Thescelosaurus is an unusual dinosaur for all sorts of reasons. Despite living toward the end of the Cretaceous Period, right before the dinosaurs were extinct, it was relatively unevolved for an ornithopod, it had short legs and four-toed feet, and had three different kinds of teeth. Judging by its anatomy, paleontologists speculate that Thescelosaurus couldn't have run very fast, and it is not known how it avoided the raptors and tyrannosaurs that populated late Cretaceous North America.

WOW FACT

What made Thescelosaurus truly famous, though, was the discovery in 1993 of an almost intact specimen containing the fossilized remains of what seemed to be a quite advanced, almost mammalian-looking four-chambered heart. The trouble is, paleontologists are now divided about whether this was really the dinosaur's heart, or some by-product of the fossilization process that has nothing to do with Thescelosaurus' anatomy. The evidence is still inconclusive.

AWESOME

Thescelosaurus was discovered in 1891. However, this dinosaur did not receive a name until 1913. After being discovered, the fossils were hidden away in a crate in the basement of the Smithsonian Institution until studied many years later by Charles Gilmore.

DIET

Plants.

DID YOU KNOW?

Small scutes running along its back would have protected it from attack.

TENONTOSAURUS

Tenontosaurus was a medium-sized bird-footed, ornithopod dinosaur. Living in the early Cretaceous Period 140 million years ago, this plant-eater spent its days crouched on all fours foraging for food, or standing on its rear legs trying to reach food high in the tree tops. Tenontosaurus was discovered in North America and named in 1970 by John Ostrom.

WOW FACT

Tenontosaurus was most interesting for its unusually long tail, which was suspended off the ground by specialized tendons, hence this dinosaur's name, which is Greek for 'tendon lizard'.

DID YOU KNOW?

Tenontosaurus probably walked on all fours and ate low-growing plants and shrubs.

WOW TASTY!

Some dinosaurs are more famous for how they got eaten than for how they actually lived. That's the case with Tenontosaurus, as it was on the lunch menu of the raptor Deinonychus. An adult Tenontosaurus was large, around 2000 pounds or 1000 kilos, smaller raptors like Deinonychus would have had to hunt in packs to bring it down.

TENONTOSAURUS STATS

PRONOUNCED:	Ten-on-toe-sore-us
MEANS:	Tendon Lizard
HEIGHT:	25 ft or 7.5 m
WEIGHT:	2000 lbs or 1000 kg

OTHNIELIA

Othnielia pronounced oth-nee-ELL-ee-ah lived during the late Jurassic Period, about 156-145 million years ago. It was an ornithopod dinosaur that measured about 4 ft or 1.1 m long, weighing about 50 lbs or 22.5 kg. Othnielia had a horny beak and a small skull with self-sharpening cheek teeth. Othnielia may have had cheek pouches.

Othnielia was a plant-eater and was bipedal (walked on two legs). It had thin legs and a stiffened tail that gave it speed and agility. It had five-fingered hands and four-toed feet, all clawed. It had large eyes and short arms. Othnielia resembled Hypsilophodon but had longer feet and different vertebrae.

DID YOU KNOW?

Othnielia was named after the 19th Century paleontologist Othniel C Marsh.

WOW, FAST!

Othnielia was a very fast runner. It had long legs with very long shins; this made it a very fast runner. Othnielia had a stiffened tail that helped it balance when running and turning. Othnielia may have lived in herds, and it certainly figured on the dinner menu of the larger, carnivorous theropods of its day, which may explain its speed and agility.

ALTIRHINUS

Altirhinus which is Greek for 'high nose' and pronounced AL-tih-RYE-nus, lived in the woodlands of Central Asia in the middle Cretaceous Period, around 125–100 million years ago. Altirhinus was a member of the Ornithopoda, or bird-foot group. These dinosaurs had feet similar to those of modern birds. In many ways this dinosaur resembled a camel.

AWESOME!

Ornithopodas are among the most successful of all dinosaur groups, living for tens of millions of years.

CONFUSED?

Altirhinus is often pointed to as evolving from two closely related dinosaur families. It has a hadrosaur-like bump on its nose, which resembles an early version of the elaborate crests of later duck-billed dinosaurs. If you ignore this growth, Altirhinus also looked a lot like Iguanodon, which is why most experts classify it as an iguanodont ornithopod rather than a true hadrosaur. In fact, in 1952 it was originally named Orientalis. As time went on, it became apparent that this dinosaur was actually a separate species and in 1998 it was renamed Altirhinus.

DRYOSAURUS

Dryosaurus pronounced dry-oh-sore-us lived during the Late Jurassic Period, 155-145 million years ago. Dryosaurus is the most important member of the family Dryosauridae.
This is a group of small plant-eating dinosaurs from the late Jurassic and early Cretaceous Period and found in North America, Eastern Africa, and Europe. Dryosaurus were about 10 ft or 3 m long and their weight was around 200 lbs or 75 kg.

WOW

Dryosaurus had long, powerful back legs. Its feet were slim and had three toes. Its arms were strong and had five-fingered hands. Its stiff tail balanced the body while it was standing or running across the countryside.

AWESOME

Dryosaurus meaning 'oak lizard,' refers to the oak-leaf-like shape of some of its teeth. Dryosaurus had no teeth at the front of its mouth. It used its horny beak to nip plants from the ground, shrubs, and low-level.

DID YOU KNOW?

Living during the Late Jurassic Period, Dryosaurus is one of the first Ornithopods to have evolved. Ornithopod means bird-footed dinosaur, which refers to the fact that the hind feet of this dinosaur were very similar to those of modern birds. Many scientists today believe that birds actually evolved from dinosaurs. Another feature that Dryosaurus had in common with modern birds was its beak. It used this beak to cut vegetation, which it then chewed using teeth located near its cheeks.

ORODROMEUS

Orodromeus pronounced ore-oh-drome-ee-us lived in the Woodlands of North America during the late Cretaceous Period around 75 million years ago. Compared to other dinosaurs, Orodromeus was rather small, it was only 10 ft or 3 m in length. Like other members of the ornithopoda group, it was a plant-eater and Orodromeus had a toothless beak that it used for cutting vegetation. Within its mouth, Orodromeus had a set of teeth used for crushing and grinding food before swallowing.

DID YOU KNOW?

The name Orodromeus means 'Mountain Jumper.' Like modern day mountain sheep, this dinosaur probably spent its life leaping about from rock to rock foraging for food.

AWESOME FACT!

The mother Orodromeus laid about 12 eggs in a tight spiral, with the first egg in the center of the spiral. These eggs were not large, almost 6 in or 15.4 cm high and around 2 3/4 in or 7 cm wide. When the embryos were ready to come out of their eggs, they pecked through the top of the shell and climbed out of the nest. These hatchlings were nearly as fully developed as adults and could leave the nest and feed themselves. Possibly for protection, these hatchlings stayed together after leaving the nest.

DISCOVERY OF FOSSILS

The best way we have of learning about dinosaurs is by discovering and studying fossils. Fossils are the remains of ancient animals and plants, the traces or impressions of living things from past geologic ages, or the traces of their activities. Fossils have been found on every continent on Earth. It is the possible to find dinosaur remains anywhere that continental rocks were deposited at the end of the Triassic and throughout the whole of the Jurassic and Cretaceous Periods. Fossil discoveries can give us lots of information about dinosaur behavior and lifestyle.

DID YOU KNOW?

Most animals don't turn into fossils, they simply decay and are lost from the fossil record. Paleontologists estimate that only a small percentage of the dinosaurs that were around will be found as fossils.

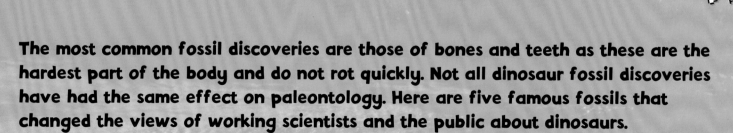

The most common fossil discoveries are those of bones and teeth as these are the hardest part of the body and do not rot quickly. Not all dinosaur fossil discoveries have had the same effect on paleontology. Here are five famous fossils that changed the views of working scientists and the public about dinosaurs.

1. MEGALOSAURUS (1676) P 68

When the partial femur of Megalosaurus was discovered in England in 1676, an Oxford University professor identified it as belonging to a giant! It took another 150 years, in 1824, for William Buckland to name it, and nearly 20 years after that for Megalosaurus to be identified as a dinosaur by Richard Owen.

2. ARCHAEOPTERYX (1860-62) P 154

Around the same time as Charles Darwin published his revolutionary work on evolution The Origin of Species, a series of spectacular discoveries in Solnhofen, Germany of an Archaeopteryx, came to light. Archaeopteryx seemed to be the perfect missing link between dinosaurs and birds. Since then, more convincing transitional fossils of Sinosauropteryx have been found, but none have had the same impact as Archaeopteryx.

3. DIPLODOCUS (1877) P 86

The discovery of Diplodocus in western North America's Morrison Formation gave rise to the identification of the giant sauropods, which really captured the public imagination to a much greater extent than previous finds like Megalosaurus and Iguanodon.

4. T-REX (1990) P 36

'Sue' is the nickname given to FMNH PR 2081, the largest, most famous and best preserved Tyrannosaurus Rex find to date. It is considered by many scientists to be the most important fossil of all time. It was discovered in 1990 by Sue Hendrickson, a paleontologist, and was named after her. Many ownership disputes were raised over this fossil, but after these were settled it was auctioned in October 1997 for US$7.6 million, the highest amount ever paid for a dinosaur fossil, and is now at the Field Museum of Natural History in Chicago, Illinois.

5. BRACHYLOPHOSAURUS (2000) P 92

Although this wasn't the first specimen of Brachylophosaurus to be discovered, it was the most spectacular. A near-complete, mummified, teenaged hadrosaur gave rise to use of new technology in paleontology, as researchers used high-powered X-rays and MRI scans in an attempt to piece together the internal anatomy. Many of these same techniques are now being applied to other dinosaur fossils.

FORMATION OF FOSSILS

A fossil means the traces of any past life preserved in rocks. Fossilization takes millions of years to happen. If a dinosaur died and was quickly covered in sediment then the chances of fossilization were high. Once the sediment covered the dinosaur's body, the flesh would quickly rot away but the bones and teeth, the hard parts of the body, would remain. As the sediment gradually built up over the body, minerals from water around the rocks would seep into the bones and gradually they would be turned into rock. Erosion from the wind and water wears rock away and exposes the dinosaur fossil, and with some luck a sharp-eyed fossil collector will find it and excavate. If not the elements will continue to erode it and it will return to sand or mud.

TYPES OF FOSSIL

Petrified fossils – when the conditions are favorable minerals seep into the bones, and gradually turn the bones into rocks. Petrifaction means to turn into a stone.

Natural mold and cast fossils – sometimes acidic water dissolves the bone and leaves a hollow space or mold where the bone would have been.

Mummified fossils – these are rarest of fossils formed when the dinosaur's body had been covered in a dry environment and some of the soft parts have become preserved (mummified) and then fossilized. In these cases the skin texture, and even the folds in it can be clearly seen.

NOT JUST BONES!

Other parts of the dinosaurs were also fossilized which helps us to understand how they lived and behaved. These include footprints, dung, and stomach stones.

DID YOU KNOW?

The word fossil comes from the Latin word fossilis which means 'dug up'.

LOST IN TIME

Paleontologists estimate that only a few of the dinosaurs that ever lived have been or will be found as fossils. Most animals did not fossilize, they simply decayed and so are lost from the fossil record.

FOSSIL FACT!

We have known about dinosaur fossils for a long time but it wasn't until the early 19th century that they were formally recognized as the dinosaurs we learn about today.

WOW FACT

Dinosaur fossils have been found on every continent of Earth, including Antarctica.

WHY DID THE DINOSAURS BECOME EXTINCT?

The dinosaurs lived for more than 150 million years and were the most successful group of animals ever. They all died out 65 million years ago, as did the flying reptiles and most of the sea reptiles. In fact 70% of all species on earth died out. This event is called the **K-T Extinction Event**. Most scientists blame a combination of two things, a meteorite hitting the earth and massive volcanic eruptions.

GREAT BALLS OF FIRE

When the meteorite hit the Earth, it made a huge explosion destroying everything. Huge dust clouds blocked the sunlight and caused massive forest fires, storms and tidal waves. The fires wiped out massive areas of plant life. At the same time volcanoes all over the planet erupted – they poured out red-hot lava (liquid rock) that burned everything it touched.

DARKNESS

After the strike, the dust clouds surrounding the Earth shut out sunlight for about six months. It became cold, dusty and dark, making it hard for animals to live and breathe. Without sunlight, plant life died and the herbivores starved and so did the carnivores that preyed on them.

THE DYING SEA

Underwater volcanoes erupted, sending water from the seabed to the surface. This deep-sea water was low in oxygen and killed most of the plankton living at the surface. The marine reptiles died because some of them fed on plankton and others fed on the plankton-eaters.

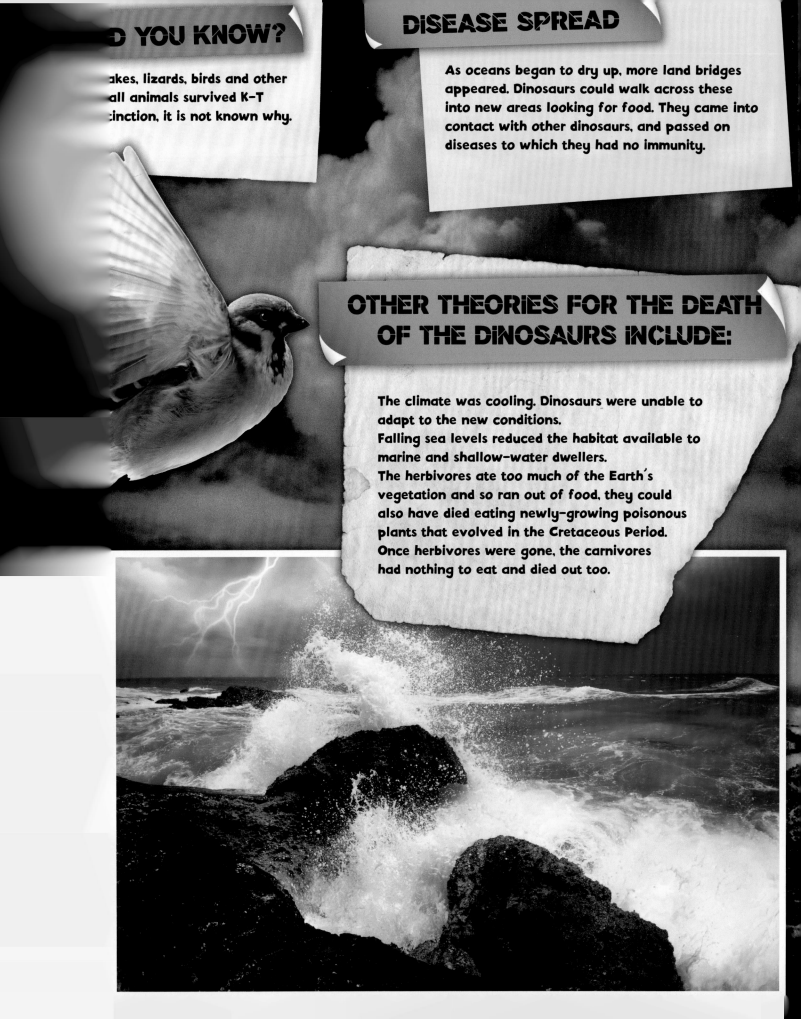

D YOU KNOW?

akes, lizards, birds and other
all animals survived K-T
tinction, it is not known why.

DISEASE SPREAD

As oceans began to dry up, more land bridges appeared. Dinosaurs could walk across these into new areas looking for food. They came into contact with other dinosaurs, and passed on diseases to which they had no immunity.

OTHER THEORIES FOR THE DEATH OF THE DINOSAURS INCLUDE:

The climate was cooling. Dinosaurs were unable to adapt to the new conditions.
Falling sea levels reduced the habitat available to marine and shallow-water dwellers.
The herbivores ate too much of the Earth's vegetation and so ran out of food, they could also have died eating newly-growing poisonous plants that evolved in the Cretaceous Period.
Once herbivores were gone, the carnivores had nothing to eat and died out too.

GLOSSARY

ammonite extinct marine molluscs, had coiled shells

ancestor animal from which a later, related animal has evolved

ankylosaurs a group of armoured herbivores that lived 76–68 million years ago.

aquatic water-dwelling

archosaurs triassic reptiles, immediate ancestors of the dinosaurs

binocular vision ability to focus on the same thing with two eyes

biped animal that walks on two hind legs

bipedal walks on two legs

camouflage coloring allowing an animal to blend in with its surroundings

carnivore a meat eater

cephalopod any mollusc of the class Cephalopoda having tentacles attached to the head including squid and octopus

ceratopsian plant-eating dinosaurs with horned faces

coelurosaurs 'hollow-tail lizards' – early members of this group were very small, but its members in the end included the most likely ancestors of modern birds

cold-blooded cold-blooded creatures rely on their environment to regulate their body temperature

conifers evergreen trees and shrubs

Cretaceous last period of the Mesozoic era, 135–65 million years ago

cycad plant like a palm tree with a middle trunk and leaves

dinosaurs land-dwelling reptiles from the Mesozoic era

erosion the wearing away of the Earth's surface by natural forces

evolution process by which one species changes into another, usually over a long period of time

extinction the process of becoming extinct, no longer existing

femur main thigh bone

fenestrae gap or holes in bone, from the Latin for windows

fern leafy plant growing in damp places

fossil remains preserved in rock

geologist person who studies rock

grazing feeding on low-growing plants

hadrosaurs duck-billed plant-eating dinosaurs

hesperornithiforms a group of dinosaurs, that were the only true marine dinosaurs.

herbivore an animal which just eats plants

horsetail primitive spore-bearing plant, common in Mesozoic era

ichthyosaurs sea-dwelling prehistoric reptiles

Jurassic period of the Mesozoic era, 203–135 million years ago

K-T Extinction Event extinction event which occurred at the end of the Cretaceous period resulting in extinction of the dinosaurs and many other species

lizard scaly-bodied, air breathing reptile with backbone that evolved from amphibians

mammal hairy warm-blooded animal that nourishes young from mammary glands and evolved during Triassic period

membrane thin layer of tissue protecting embryo in egg

Mesozoic era age of reptiles, 248–65 million years ago which includes Triassic, Jurassic and Cretaceous periods

mosasaurs types of marine reptiles

omnivore animal which eats a mixed diet of plants and meat

ornithopods beaked, usually bipedal, plant-eating dinosaurs that flourished from the late Triassic to the late Cretaceous (ornithopod means bird feet)

orthacanthus a primitive shark

ossicles pea-sized bones

paleontologist person who studies fossils

Pangaea the 'super-continent' formed of all Earth's land masses

paravertebrae extra bony plates added to backbone of dinosaur

plesiosaurs large marine reptiles that lived in Mesozoic era (not dinosaurs)

predator animal which hunts other animals to eat

primitive basic, at an early stage of development

pterandons a group of flying reptiles that were usually toothless and had a short tail

pterodophytes a type of fern (a plant)

pterosaurs flying prehistoric reptiles (not dinosaurs but lived at the same time)

quadruped animal that walks on all fours

rhynchosaurs herbivorous reptiles from Mezozoic era

sauropods giant, plant-eating dinosaurs with long neck, small head and long tail

scavenger animal that feeds on (dead) meat which it finds, rather than hunts

scutes bony protective plates offering defense against attack

semi-bipedal sometimes walks on hind legs, at other times walks on all fours

species a category of living things, plants or animals, refers to related living things capable of breeding with one another to produce young

stegosaurs a group of herbivorous dinosaurs of the Jurassic and early Cretaceous periods, predominantly living in North America and China.

tendons connect muscle to bone

territory the land or area where an animal lives

theropods fast moving, bipedal carnivores with grasping hands and claws

Triassic first period of the Mesozoic era, 248–203 million years ago

vertebrae the bones which are linked together to make the spine of an animal

warm-blooded able to keep the body at constant temperature, regardless of the environment

GLOSSARY CONTINUED

rhynchosaurs herbivorous reptiles from Mezozoic era

sauropods giant, plant-eating dinosaurs with long neck, small head and long tail

scavenger animal that feeds on (dead) meat which it finds, rather than hunts

scutes bony protective plates offering defense against attack

semi-bipedal sometimes walks on hind legs, at other times walks on all fours

species a category of living things, plants or animals, refers to related living things capable of breeding with one another to produce young

stegosaurs a group of herbivorous dinosaurs of the Jurassic and early Cretaceous periods, predominantly living in North America and China.

tendons connect muscle to bone

territory the land or area where an animal lives

theropods fast moving, bipedal carnivores with grasping hands and claws

Triassic first period of the Mesozoic era, 248–203 million years ago

vertebrae the bones which are linked together to make the spine of an animal

warm-blooded able to keep the body at constant temperature, regardless of the environment

INDEX

BEHIND THE SCENES

Some of the artwork in this book looks real as if we had gone back in time and photographed it – we wish!

We have used the latest 3D modelling technology and all of the dinosaurs have been built as 3D, Computer Generated Images, CGI, models, just like you see in Jurassic park and most of the Monsters and special effects in films.

Each 3D Dinosaur is built from scratch on a computer and once finished is alive within the computer monitor, it's arms can move, legs can move and it can be animated to run around and roar loudly.

Below is a basic 4 step guide to how we create our dinosaur images.

1. 'We start by creating a basic mesh (outline) this is a mathematical Polygon, and are the building blocks for the dinosaur.

3. We then start to apply skin to the model using digital sculpting.

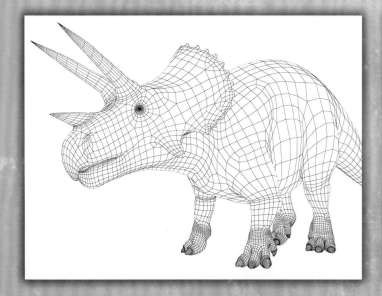

2. Then we start to create the physical structure of the bones using curve modelling.

4. Finally we render the model into a flat image ready to appear in this book.

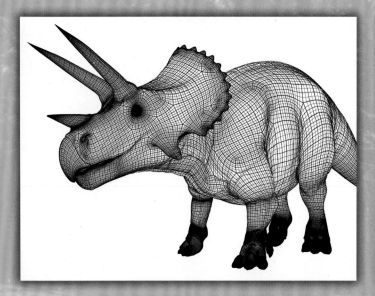